Catherine Guidicelli

MY FIRST SEWING

BOOK

Learn how to sew
by **HAND** and **MACHINE**

DOVER PUBLICATIONS, INC.
Mineola, New York

Acknowledgments

The author and the publisher would like to thank Linna Morata, who graciously provided most of the fabrics needed to make the models for this book.
www.linnamorata.com

Credits

Artistic Direction: Thérèse Jauze
Graphic Production: Magali Meunier
Photographs: Charlotte Brunet
Illustrations: Catherine Guidicelli
Patterns according to fabrics: Laurent Stefano

Bibliographical Note

This Dover edition, first published in 2018, is a new English translation of the work originally published in French by Fleurus Editions, Paris, in 2017, under the title *Mes premiers ateliers de couture: Pour apprendre à coudre à la main et à la machine*. Since the diagrams within the book contain metric measurements, a conversion chart has been provided on page 240.

International Standard Book Number

ISBN-13: 978-0-486-82909-8
ISBN-10: 0-486-82909-X

Manufactured in the United States by LSC Communications
82909X01   2018
www.doverpublications.com

Welcome
to the wonderful world
of sewing!

In recent years, sewing has been gaining more and more fans among both children and adults. Maybe you would like to give it a try, too!
If a family member or someone else you know already sews, you of course have someone to help you. You may also take regular classes or participate in a special workshop to get started.

This book, which explains all of the basics and puts them directly into practice through simple creations, will be an ideal companion to guide you through your first steps. It will allow you to understand the different techniques, choose fabrics and use your materials well. It lists everything you need to know, down to the smallest details. Read the introduction for an overview of the basics, and return to it regularly while you are sewing.

The list of supplies may seem long. When stored properly and used carefully, the contents of your sewing box will last a long time and are often handed down from one generation to the next! Don't be discouraged if the techniques seem difficult at first! In reality, sewing often boils down to a few basic points and major principles that are found across many projects.
Keep telling yourself that sewing is a bit like riding a bicycle...
Once you know how to pedal without the training wheels, you never forget.

To your needle and thread!

Contents

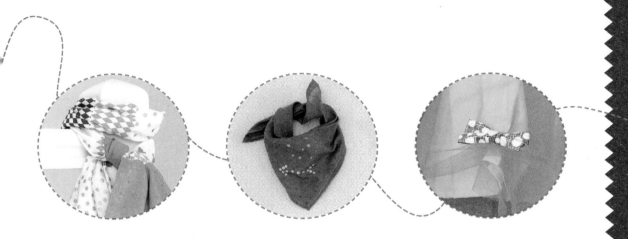

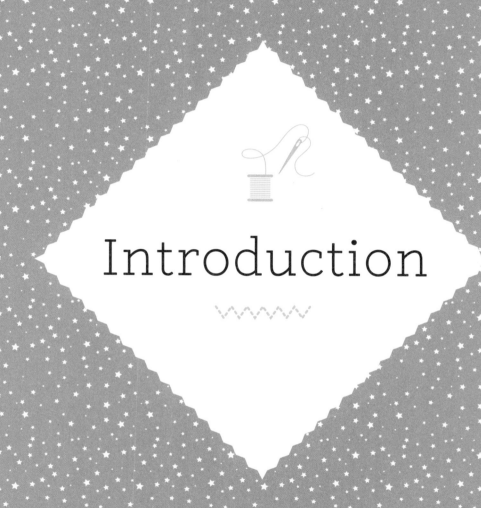

Introduction

Materials

Your sewing box
You will use these basic materials for all of your projects.

A **pair of true sewing shears.** These must be used for cutting fabric only. Otherwise, they will lose their sharpness. One of the blades is generally pointed, and the other is more rounded. Customize them, for example with a small piece of tape, so that you will recognize them.

A **seam ripper** or pair of small, **pointy embroidery scissors** for cutting threads and unstitching.

A **tape measure** for measuring.

A **black grease pencil** (2B) for drawing on paper and light fabrics.

A **white chalk pencil** (from the fabric store) for drawing on dark fabrics.

Straight pins. These are used to keep layers of fabric together. Preferably, choose the ones with colored heads. They will be easy to see against the fabrics or if you drop them.

Sewing needles with medium thicknesses. Avoid needles that are too thin to thread easily.

A **needle threader**. This is not required but is very useful for threading needles. All you need to do is slip the flexible metal loop through the eye (hole) of the needle, place the thread in the loop, then gently pull the flat part in order to pull the thread through the eye.

Several spools of **sewing thread**. You do not need a very wide variety of threads to get started: white or ecru for light fabrics and black for dark fabrics may be enough to begin. For visible stitches (those which you will be able to see on the front side of the project), it is preferable to choose a thread that matches the dominant color of the fabric.

Try to purchase high-quality "all textiles" threads, all by the same brand, so that they can be used together without problems in the sewing machine. Avoid thread lots. They are not expensive, but their poor quality does not allow correct sewing.

Depending on the projects, you may also need additional supplies.

Embroidery needles. These have a slightly wider eye (hole) than sewing needles to allow a thicker thread to pass.

Safety pins

Other common materials
To produce the patterns, you will need:

Paper and **tracing paper**

A **ruler** from 12 in. (30 cm) to 20 in. (50 cm)

A **square**

A **pair of paper scissors** (which you will reserve for this use)

Sewing machine

A simple machine will suffice. If you are buying one, choose one that is not too heavy and is compact, but solid. Sewing machine manufacturers offer many models for beginners, with the essential functions.

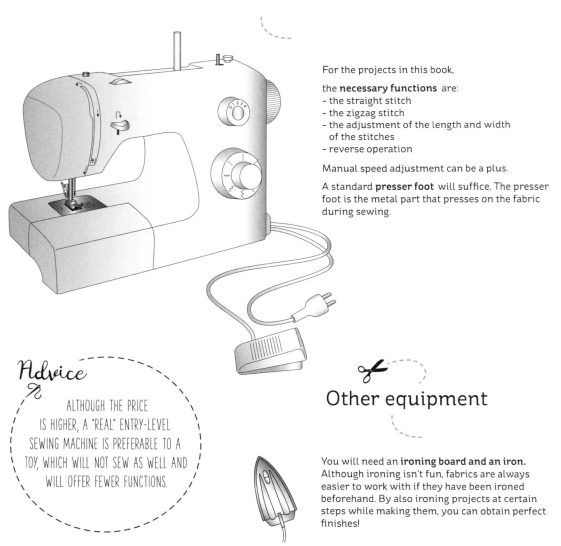

For the projects in this book,

the **necessary functions** are:
- the straight stitch
- the zigzag stitch
- the adjustment of the length and width
  of the stitches
- reverse operation

Manual speed adjustment can be a plus.

A standard **presser foot** will suffice. The presser foot is the metal part that presses on the fabric during sewing.

Advice

ALTHOUGH THE PRICE IS HIGHER, A "REAL" ENTRY-LEVEL SEWING MACHINE IS PREFERABLE TO A TOY, WHICH WILL NOT SEW AS WELL AND WILL OFFER FEWER FUNCTIONS.

Other equipment

You will need an **ironing board and an iron.** Although ironing isn't fun, fabrics are always easier to work with if they have been ironed beforehand. By also ironing projects at certain steps while making them, you can obtain perfect finishes!

Fabrics

Choosing a fabric and imagining the project that you will make with it
are among the greatest pleasures in sewing!

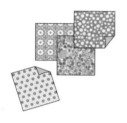

Cotton fabrics with an average thickness intended for clothing are the easiest to sew. The majority of the projects in this book use them.
Avoid heavy patterns. Plain fabrics or fabrics with small patterns are easier to work with, since you do not need to worry about how the patterns will be placed or how they will connect on the finished project.

Some of the projects in this book are made with **special fabrics**, such as tulle, coated fabric, denim or fake fur. Choose them when you feel more comfortable sewing.

Fabrics to avoid

Linen, jersey (T-shirt), nylon, lining fabric, wool, voile, etc., and any fabrics that are too thick or too thin, too slippery, that fray or that wrinkle too easily. They are difficult to sew or maintain (and sometimes both at the same time!).

Trick

GET IN THE HABIT OF
KEEPING BUTTONS, PIECES OF
RIBBON OR CLOTHING YOU DON'T WEAR
ANYMORE BUT THE FABRIC OF WHICH YOU
LIKE: YOU MAY BE ABLE TO USE THEM
TO CUSTOMIZE YOUR PROJECTS.

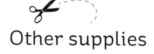

Other supplies

Piping, **string**, **buttons** necessary to decorate certain models.

Synthetic filling
to give volume to certain creations.

Embroidery thread

Bits of **wool** that you will use to make pompoms.

Heat-activated interfacing
to stiffen the fabric.

Fabric

Buy the right amount

The amount of fabric to buy is stated in the instructions.
Most of the time, the fabric is sold "by the yard." The length
to be purchased is defined by multiples of 4 in. (10 cm). The minimum purchase
length varies depending on the seller. The width of the fabrics is most often
comprised between 43 in. and 59 in. (110 cm and 150 cm). As a result, sometimes
you will have too much fabric. You will also find remnants measuring about 18 x 20
in. (45 x 50 cm), which are perfect for small accessories.

Before you cut

Wash the fabric by hand, in hot water. This will prevent it from shrinking
or bleeding after it is sewn.
Iron the fabric so that you can cut it straight. To do this, spread the fabric out on the
ironing board. Set your iron's temperature based on the quality of the fabric. Move the
iron regularly over the entire surface of the fabric, slowly, without stopping. You do not
need to press hard; the weight of the iron is enough.

Characteristics of fabric

The fabrics have a back side and a front side.
The back side is generally lighter.
It is shown in gray in the drawings in this book.
The fiber direction or grain direction corresponds to the direction of the weaving.
The selvages are the uncut sides (between the two selvages is the width of the fabric).
Do not use them, since they are stiff and often printed with text. However, use them
as a guide to draw your pieces. The fiber direction is parallel to the selvages; the bias
is 45° to that.

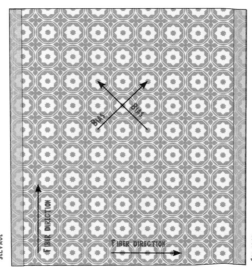

Place the pattern pieces carefully on the fabric

If you have several pieces to cut from the fabric,
draw all of them before you cut to be sure that you have enough fabric.
A **cutting guide** will tell you how to arrange them to prevent loss.

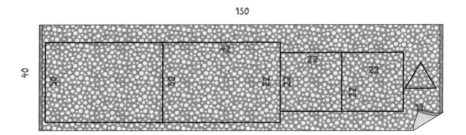

Place your pieces in the fiber direction so that they
will not deform. If you cut them on the bias,
they will be elastic and difficult to sew.

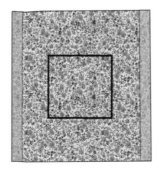 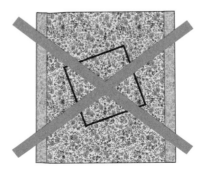

The patterns of the fabric are not always parallel to the selvage. You may sometimes take this into account to place your pieces, as long as you do not deviate too much from the fiber direction.

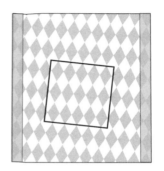

If you have a single piece to cut from an overly large piece of fabric, do not place it in the middle, but in a corner of the fabric.
That way you will have some left over for another time!

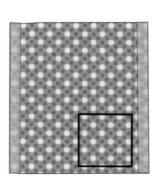 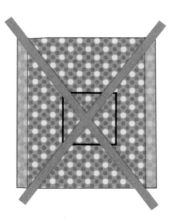

Patterns

A pattern is the paper model of the fabric piece
to be cut. You will find patterns at the end of the book.

Using an actual-size pattern

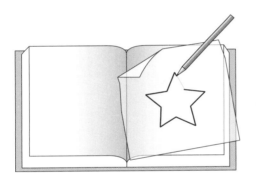

With tracing paper, simply trace
the pattern, following the outlines carefully.

Enlarging a pattern

1. Trace the pattern on the paper with a ruler and a square. A grid and dimensions will tell you how to trace it.
First, use the ruler and the square to copy the grid: 1 square = 2 in. (5 cm.)

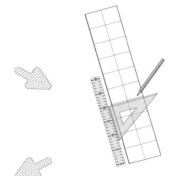

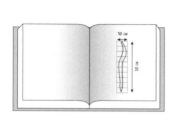

2. Draw the pattern in the grid, square by square, following the model.

Half-pattern

For some symmetrical pieces, a half-pattern has been drawn. Fold your paperin half and align the half-pattern against the crease.
Unfold after cutting to obtain the full pattern.

Drawing on fabric

Spread your fabric out on a large table, after clearing the table.

Straight shapes without pattern

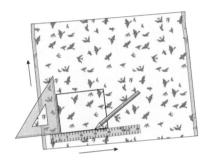

Trace directly on the fabric with the ruler and square, placing them in the fiber direction, i.e., parallel and perpendicular to the selvage. In the drawing, the arrows show you the fiber direction.

With a pattern

First method

1. Turn over the copy you have already made of the pattern and trace the back side of the pattern on tracing paper, using a grease pencil.

2. Place the pattern on the front side of the fabric with the grease-pencil side down and trace the pattern again. The one on the back side will be transferred to the fabric.

This method is reserved for small pieces to be traced on light fabrics.

You do not need to copy the pattern onto the back if it is symmetrical. In this case, draw the pattern directly with the grease pencil.

Second method

1. Cut out the transferred shape. Place the pattern on the fabric and pin it. Place the pins inside the outline. Following the contour of the pattern, draw it on the fabric using the grease pencil. Remove the pins, then cut.

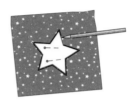

2. You can also cut the fabric directly around the pattern without tracing it.

This second method is recommended for large pieces and fabrics with denser colors or patterns. If the fabric is very dark, trace the pattern outline with the white pencil.

To cut well

Trick

SOMETIMES IT IS PREFERABLE TO DRAW ON THE BACK OF THE FABRIC SO YOU CAN SEE BETTER. PAY ATTENTION TO THE DIRECTION OF THE PIECE IF THE PATTERN IS NOT SYMMETRICAL.

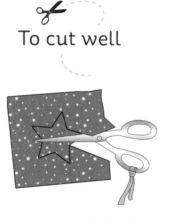

Hold your scissors straight by placing the pointy blade on top. Cut with the bottom of the blades rather than the tips. If it is large, hold the fabric on the table with the other hand.

Sewing by hand

Preparing the needle

Here, the thread refers to the length of thread on the needle.

Choose the thread closest in color to your fabric.
Otherwise, choose a white or ecru thread for light fabrics
and a black thread for dark fabrics.

Unless another length is indicated, cut a maximum of 12 to 16 in.
(30 to 40 cm) of thread. Any longer and the thread will tangle.
If necessary, cut the end of the thread again, more cleanly, and wet
it between your lips to make it stiffer. Hold this end between the
thumb and index finger of one hand and push it into the eye of the
needle that you are holding in your other hand. Allow 4 in. (10 cm)
to pass to the other side of the needle.

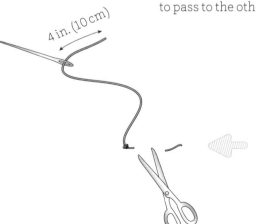

4 in. (10 cm)

At the other end of the thread, make two or
three knots on top of one another. A single knot
would be too small and would pass through the
fabric. Cut the thread again ⅛ in. (3 mm) away
from the knot.

To start, unless otherwise indicated, pull the
needle through from the back of the fabric
until you reach the knot.

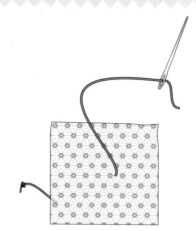

Trick

WHEN YOU SEW,
THE THREAD MAY SLIP OFF THE
NEEDLE. HOLD THE NEEDLE CLOSE TO
THE EYE AND HOLD BOTH STRANDS
BETWEEN YOUR FINGERS.

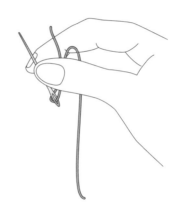

Finishing a length of thread

To finish a length of thread when the seam is complete or when
you do not have enough thread to continue, make several small stitches on
top of one another on the back side of the fabric.

Hand stitches

Unless otherwise indicated, make regular stitches ³⁄₁₆ in. (5 mm) long.

Depending on the selected stitch, the seam will be made from right to left or from left to right. The illustrations here are shown as if they would be stitched by right-handed sewers. If you are left-handed, reverse the direction. You can look at the drawings in a mirror for greater ease.

Running stitch
from right to left

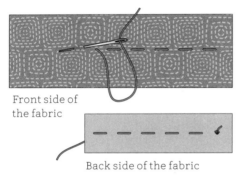

Front side of the fabric

Back side of the fabric

This stitch is used to baste (sew temporarily to keep two pieces of fabric together) and place gathering threads. It is also used for embroidery.

To work more quickly and produce more regular stitches, insert the needle into the fabric several times before pulling the thread through.

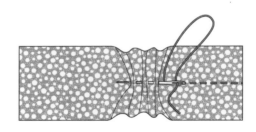

Front side of the fabric

Reverse stitch
from right to left

This stitch is used for assembly.

Back side of the fabric

Lock stitch
from right to left

This stitch is used for assembly, like the reverse stitch, but the stitches are adjacent and more solid.

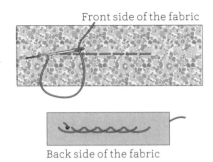

Front side of the fabric

Back side of the fabric

Overcast stitch
from left to right

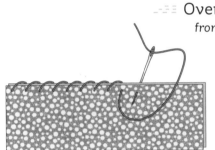

This stitch is used to close an opening.

Slip stitch or hemstitch
from right to left

You will need this to shorten pants, for example.

Hold the project so that the hem is at the top. Remove the needle just below the hem and insert it even with the hem.

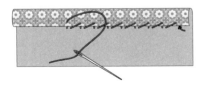

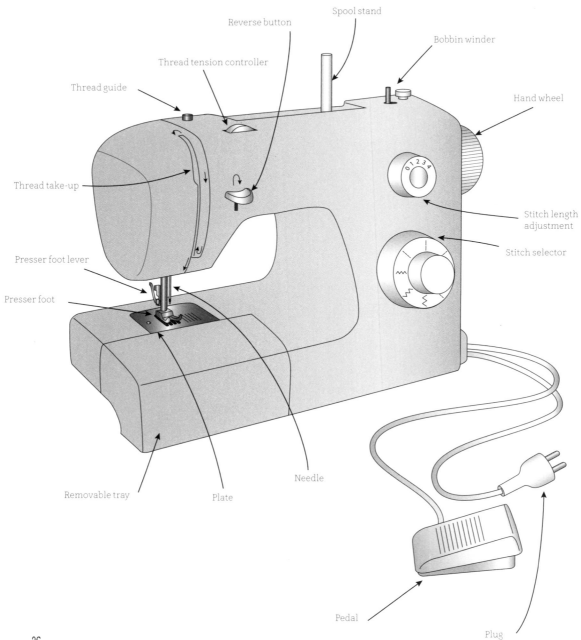

Reverse button

Spool stand

Bobbin winder

Thread tension controller

Thread guide

Hand wheel

Thread take-up

Stitch length adjustment

Stitch selector

Presser foot lever

Presser foot

Needle

Removable tray

Plate

Pedal

Plug

Sewing with the machine

Introduction to the machine

The drawing shows the main parts of the machine. They may look different from one machine to another. To identify them properly, also look at the instructions from your machine's manufacturer.

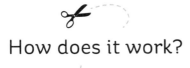

How does it work?

The machine sews with two threads: the one from the main spool and the one from the bobbin. The bobbin is a mini spool made from plastic or metal. The thread from the spool starts from the top of the machine and passes through various levers that stretch it, then through the needle. The thread from the bobbin is located below the plate of the machine, inside the machine. When you press on the pedal, the motor is turned on. The needle is lowered and passes through the fabric, then the plate of the machine, and the two threads cross and form a stitch. On the fabric, you see the thread from the spool. Under the fabric, you see the thread from the bobbin.

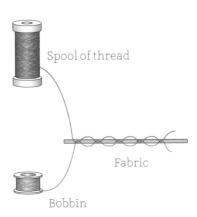

Spool of thread

Fabric

Bobbin

Preparing the bobbin

Empty bobbins are provided with the machine, and you must prepare them yourself with the thread from your spool. If you sew a lot, it is a good idea to get some extra bobbins from the fabric store so that you have one per thread color.

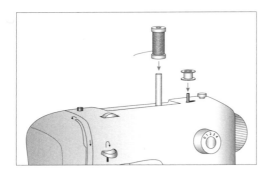

1. Place the spool on its holder. Place the bobbin on the winder and draw the thread through the provided path. Wind the thread around the bobbin about ten times, until the thread is held (in the direction indicated in the manufacturer's instructions).

2. Shift the winder to the right. Turn the wheel to lock it and press down on the pedal. The thread will automatically wind around the bobbin.

When you have filled the bobbin, place the winder back to the left and cut the thread. Don't forget to unlock the wheel!

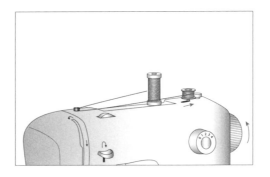

> ### ✂ Attention
> THE THREAD ON THE BOBBIN MUST BE THE SAME TYPE AS THAT ON THE SPOOL TO PREVENT PROBLEMS (KNOTTING!). IF YOU WISH TO USE TWO DIFFERENT COLORS, CHOOSE THREADS WITH THE SAME BRAND AND QUALITY.

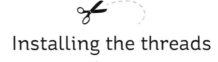

Installing the threads

Place the bobbin in its housing and close the housing cover. Raise the needle all the way. Place the spool on its holder and draw the thread through the path provided by the manufacturer. Thread it through the needle (using the same approach as for sewing by hand). Pull it to exceed 8 in. (20 cm). Turn the wheel to find the thread from the bobbin.

Note

THE NEEDLE MUST BE APPROPRIATE FOR THE THICKNESS OF THE FABRIC TO BE SEWN. A SCREW ALLOWS THE NEEDLE TO BE REMOVED AND CHANGED. THE NEEDLES HAVE NUMBERS. NEEDLE NUMBER 60 OR 70 IS USED FOR THIN FABRICS AND NEEDLE NUMBER 100 IS USED FOR THICK FABRICS. THE NEEDLE MUST ALSO BE CHANGED IF IT BECOMES BENT OR ITS TIP IS NO LONGER SHARP.

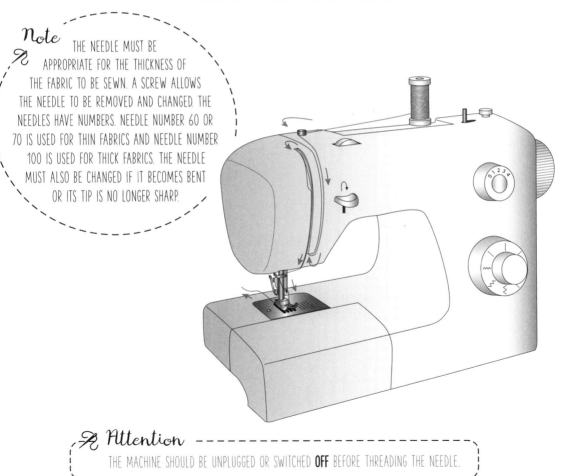

Attention

THE MACHINE SHOULD BE UNPLUGGED OR SWITCHED **OFF** BEFORE THREADING THE NEEDLE.

Choosing the stitch

The basic stitches are the **straight stitch (or lock stitch)** for assembling and the **zigzag stitch** for overcasting (bordering fabrics to prevent them from fraying) or decorating. Other stitches exist on higher-level machines.
Refer to the instructions to use them.

Stitch button   Length button

Choose your stitch and adjust its length and width. Avoid touching the tension button so you don't disrupt the settings on your machine.

Straight stitch (or lock stitch)

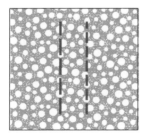

Choose an intermediate stitch length or sewing length. This stitch is also used for gathers.

Zigzag stitch

This is used for overcasting, decorating or making a more solid seam, for example for attaching the ends of an elastic band. You can vary its width and its length.

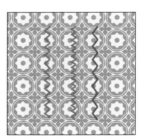

If you use this very tight stitch, you will get an embroidery-like appearance, but this uses a lot of thread.

Backstitches

They replace the knots at the beginning and end of the seam.

For the straight stitch

At the beginning of sewing, make three running stitches, three backstitches by pressing on the reverse button, then resume your running stitch.
In the sketches, the backstitches are offset so you can see them clearly.
In reality, they should be superimposed.

   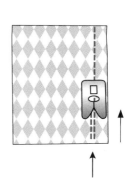

At the end, make three backstitches on the seam.

For the zigzag stitch

Make several very tight stitches at the beginning and end of the seam.

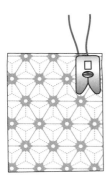 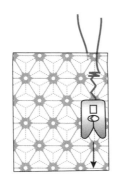

WHAT IS THE TENSION?

The tension is adjusted correctly when the thread from the spool and the thread from the bobbin cross while forming equivalent loops (see drawing). If one pulls more than the other, the seam will not be solid and the thread may break. Ask an experienced person to check the tension if you think there may be a problem.

Placing the fabric on the machine

Clear the work surface around the machine so you can spread out the fabric.

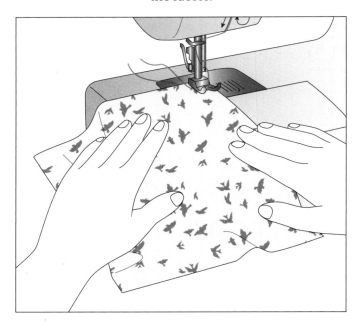

Advice

IF THE MACHINE DOES NOT ADVANCE, FIRST MAKE SURE IT IS PLUGGED IN AND POWERED ON! WHEN YOU STOP SEWING (TO MOVE YOUR FABRIC, FOR EXAMPLE) OR IF SOMEONE OR SOMETHING BREAKS YOUR CONCENTRATION, TAKE YOUR FOOT OFF THE PEDAL TO PREVENT ACCIDENTS!

Raise the needle, and raise the presser foot with the lever. Place the fabric on the plate. Place the beginning of the part to be sewn on the plate and the rest in front of it. The machine will move the fabric away as the sewing is done.

Unless otherwise indicated, place the front side facing up, since the top seam will be better placed and cleaner. Lower the presser foot again to lock the fabric in place. Place the free threads at the back.

Beginning the seam

Lower the needle into the fabric by turning the hand wheel, and hold the fabric lightly with your left hand. In this way, make a few stitches to begin the seam slowly. Next, gradually press down on the pedal. Do not pull on the fabric. It is moved automatically by the plate. Do not go too quickly. To stop, release the pedal.

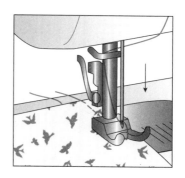

Removing the fabric from the machine

When finished, turn the hand wheel to raise the needle all the way. Raise the presser foot. Move the fabric away, then cut the threads, leaving a tail of 4 in. (10 cm). Remove the fabric and cut the threads again, against the fabric (unless otherwise indicated).

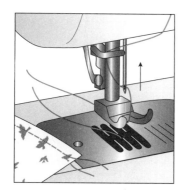

Guiding the fabric

Let the machine move the fabric. Use your hands to guide it, but always be careful not to slow it down. In this way, you can make sure that the stitches you wish to sew do not become uneven, tangled, or broken.

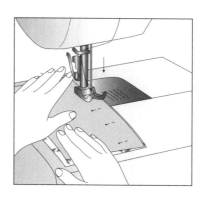

Sewing straight

With a little bit of practice, you will quickly learn to sew straight.
Follow these tips and practice on scraps of fabric.

 You can use a pencil to draw a line along the margin you need to leave yourself, generally ⅜ in. (1 cm), to help you. When you sew, you should always see the line in the center of the presser foot.

There are often reference marks provided on the plate. Align the edge of the fabric against the right reference mark, depending on the margin to be left. If the machine does not have reference marks, you can stick a piece of masking tape in the appropriate place.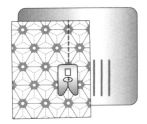

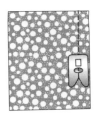 If no margin is specified or if you are more comfortable with this technique, place the edge of the presser foot against the edge of the fabric.
The margin will be about ¼ in. (0.7 cm).

Some fabric prints may also help you sew straight!

Sewing straight on curves

If the edge of the part to be sewn is rounded, guide the fabric with the left hand so that the edge of the fabric always follows the reference mark that you have chosen. This is often easier if you have chosen to align the fabric against the presser foot.

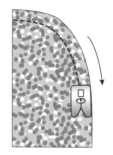

Turning corners

1. To turn a corner, stop sewing ⅜ in. (1 cm) before the edge (or a little less if you are using the presser foot as reference). Raise the presser foot, leaving the needle planted in the fabric.

2. Rotate the fabric.

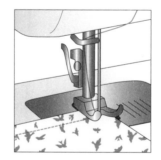

3. Lower the presser foot again and resume sewing.

Tips and tricks

WHEN YOU WISH TO CARRY OUT A PRECISE DETAIL, ACTIVATE THE MACHINE WITH THE WHEEL TO ADVANCE SLOWLY. IF THE MACHINE IS NOT SEWING OR IF IT IS MAKING KNOTS, THE THREADS FROM THE SPOOL OR THE BOBBIN ARE ALMOST CERTAINLY THREADED INCORRECTLY. BEFORE SEWING, ALWAYS PERFORM SOME TEST STITCHES ON A SCRAP OF THE SAME FABRIC.

The ABCs of sewing

Front to front

You will see this term a lot.
It means that you place the two fabrics to be sewn against each other, with the front side of one against the front side of the other.
The back is then facing you.

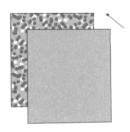

Pinning

Pins are used to hold two pieces of fabric together before they are assembled, or to hold a pattern on the fabric before cutting it out. Place the pins inside the piece, perpendicular to the seam. You can sew directly with the machine: the presser foot will pass over the tips of the pins.

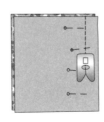

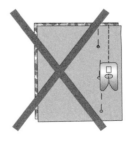

 To pin a pattern, place the pins so as to hold the ends of the pattern.

Basting

Basting is used to hold pieces more precisely than pins, before permanently sewing them.

Assemble the pieces with pins. With a contrasting colored thread, make a seam by hand, using a running stitch. Make this seam with large stitches, at least ¼ in. (6 mm) from the final seam line.

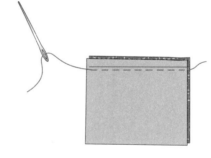

Trick

YOU CAN SKIP BASTING, ESPECIALLY ON STRAIGHT LINES, ONCE YOU'RE COMFORTABLE. IF YOU ARE SEWING A LONG LENGTH, YOU CAN DO IT BY HAND OR ON THE MACHINE WITHOUT BASTING, AFTER PINNING.

Next, make the final seam, several millimeters from the basting stitch. Remove the basting thread once the seam is complete.

Removing a seam

To remove the basting stitch or if your seam is bad, you will need to unstitch.

Advice

A SEAM MADE USING THE SEWING MACHINE TAKES LONGER TO UNSTITCH THAN TO STITCH! IF YOU MAKE A MISTAKE, BE PATIENT.

With the seam ripper, cut the stitches at regular intervals by carefully placing the tip underneath them.
Pull the threads out as you go.

Flattening (or crushing) the seams

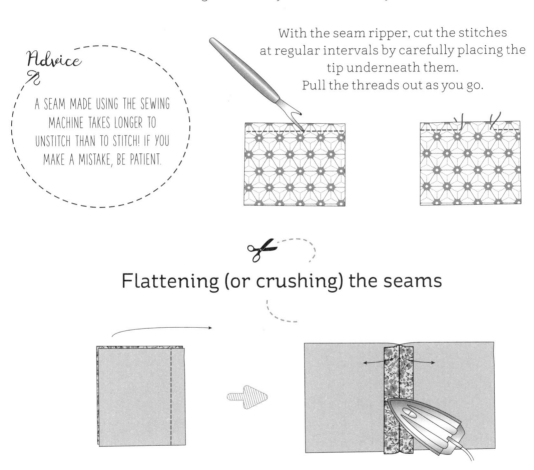

After sewing two pieces together, if instructed in the explanation, separate the two sides of the fabric and flatten the margins of the seam with your fingernail, then optionally with an iron. In this way, the margins of the seam will be well distributed and avoid excess thicknesses.

Notching

The fabric in the corners and on curves will create ripples in the finished project if we do not do something. It is therefore necessary to remove a little fabric from the margin of the seam. This is called notching.

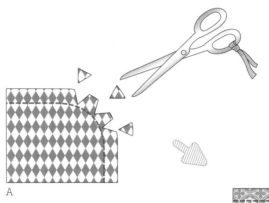

A

After making the seam, make V-shaped notches on the rounded parts (A) or cut the corners on an angle, ensuring that you do not touch the seam (B). In the hollow areas, make a few slits or else the fabric will pull (C).

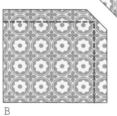

B

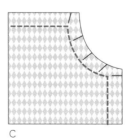

C

Making a hem

The hem makes it possible to give a clean finish to the open edge of a project (the bottom of pants or a skirt, the top of a bag, etc.).

To make a hem, you will need to make two hem folds of the same height (for example, of ⅜ or ⅝ in. [1 or 1.5 cm]).

⅜ in. or ⅝ in.
(1 cm or 1.5 cm)
⅜ in. or ⅝ in.
(1 cm or 1.5 cm)

1. Use a pencil to draw reference marks along the length of the hem to help you.

2. Fold the fabric on the reference marks and press down the fold with your fingernail.

3. Fold the fabric a second time.

4. Place pins perpendicularly or baste the hem using a slip stitch (see page 25), or using the machine.

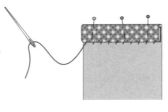
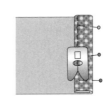

Making gathers

To make gathers, you need a fairly thin fabric. You can make gathers using the machine (required for long lengths) or by hand.

By hand

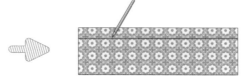

1. Using a pencil, draw a line.
2. Take a length of thread slightly longer than the fabric to be gathered and make a seam using the running stitch on the line. Do not make knots, and leave 4 in. (10 cm) of thread at the beginning and end of the seam.

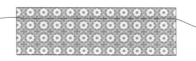

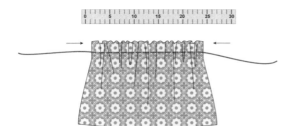

3. Pull on the thread on both ends and push the fabric toward the middle. Distribute the gathers. Measure the length of the gathered fabric based on the length you wish to obtain and correct it by sliding the fabric along the thread. Anchor the thread by making several small stitches on top of one another at the ends.

Using the machine

For small lengths of fabric, make one stitch with the running stitch adjusted to the maximum length, like for gathers done by hand.

Do not make backstitches, and leave 4 in. (10 cm) of thread at the beginning and end of the seam. Once the fabric is gathered, pull the thread backwards to bring it in front and make several knots with both threads (at each end of the gathers).

For greater regularity and over a longer length, make two parallel stitches separated by ⅜ in. (1 cm). The approach is explained for one of the projects in the book (Tutu-style skirt, page 200).

Sewing piping

Piping is a ribbon specially designed for bordering a fabric.

Since it is cut into the bias of the fabric, it is flexible and hugs all of the contours well, even rounded ones. It includes three folding lines that make it easy to place. The piping is fastened by two seams.

1. Open the piping and pin it, front to front, on the fabric, aligning the edges. Baste it on the first folding line.

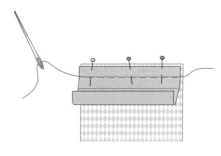

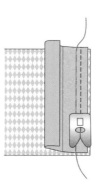

2. Remove the pins and stitch slightly above the folding line.

3. Undo the baste and re-fold the piping on the back of the fabric. Baste it. Since the first seam is hidden slightly above the fold, the crease remains very clean.

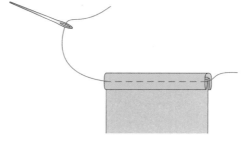

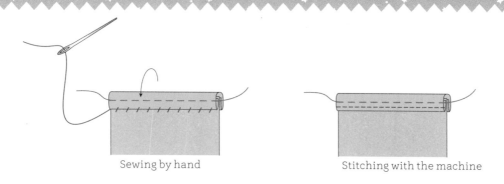

Sewing by hand   Stitching with the machine

4. Sew the piping by hand using a hemstitch, or
with the machine, close to the edge. Undo the baste.

In rounded areas

Stretch the piping slightly.
Its elasticity allows it to hug
the curves well.

To shorten piping

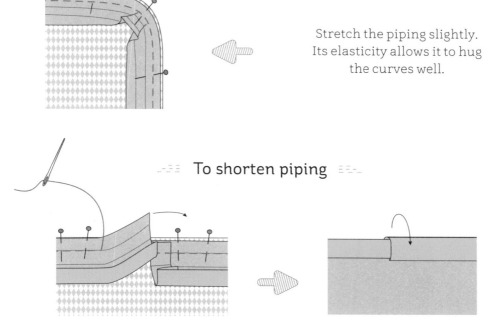

When the piping goes around a piece, fold the beginning over
⅜ in. (1 cm), then superimpose the end over ⅜ in. (1 cm).

Turning a project right-side out

Since the various pieces of fabric making up a project are most often assembled front to front, the back side is facing out once the seam is done. It is therefore necessary to turn the project right-side out to continue the assembly or to finish it.

It may also be necessary to turn it inside out again to continue.

Turning a tube right-side out

1. Tubes are found in many projects (scrunchies, headbands, bag handles, etc.). Depending on the project, they are made up of two bands assembled front to front or one band folded front to front and sewn. Once sewn, the tubes are therefore inside out, and the narrower they are, the more difficult they are to turn right-side out without a little trick!

2. Stick a safety pin in the end, but not too close to the edge so you don't destroy the fabric.

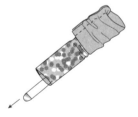

3. Place the safety pin in the tube and push it inside.

4. The fabric will crease as you go. Pull on it gently while pushing the pin inside the tube.

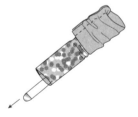

5. The inside of the tube will appear at the other end. Pull it completely. The tube is right-side out.

6. Iron the tube.

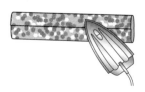

Finishing touches and decorative details

Sewing buttons

--= Buttons with two holes =--

1. For greater solidity, sew your buttons with double thread. Take a thread 23 ½ in. (60 cm) long. Fold it in half and pass the loop through the eye of the needle, up to 4 in. (10 cm) from the end.

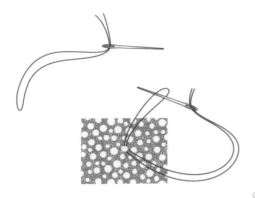

2. Make a stitch in the fabric at the location for the button and pass the needle through the loop: the thread is anchored.

3. Position the button on the fabric and pass the needle through a hole until you reach the end of the thread. Pass the needle through the second hole and through the fabric. Pull the thread on the back side.

4. Go through the other side of the fabric and the other hole. Repeat the operation two or three more times and anchor the thread on the back side by making several stitches on top of one another.

Buttons with four holes

To sew a button with four holes,
use the same approach.
Choose the arrangement of the stitches:
parallel, an "x", or square.

Buttons with shank

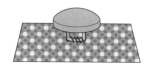

To sew a button with a shank, make three
or four stitches straddling the shank,
stitching as close as possible to the material.

SEAMSTRESS'S TRICK

On a thick piece of clothing, the button
should not be pressed against the fabric.
To loosen it, so that it is easy to pass it
through the buttonhole, wind the thread
around the stitches below the button
several times before anchoring the
thread on the back.

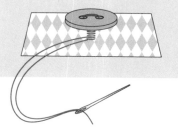

Trick

WHEN YOU
MUST REPLACE A BUTTON
ON A PIECE OF CLOTHING, POSITION
THE BUTTONHOLE ON THE FABRIC
UNDERNEATH IN THE CORRECT LOCATION.
USE YOUR PENCIL TO MAKE A
REFERENCE MARK IN THE CENTER
OF THE BUTTONHOLE.

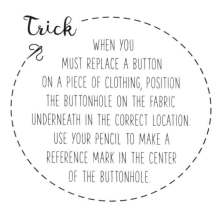

Sewing a sequin or small bead

1. Prepare a single length of thread with a knot at the end. Pull the needle through the front side of the fabric, pass it through the bead or sequin, pass it back through to the underside of the fabric and pull on the thread.

2. Repeat the operation several times, placing the stitches on top of one another.

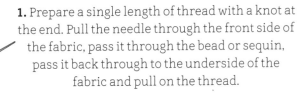

Trick

USE A RELATIVELY THIN NEEDLE FOR BEADS. POUR SEVERAL BEADS INTO A SMALL DISH. THEY WILL BE EASIER TO CATCH WITH THE NEEDLE.

Sewing a row of sequins or small beads

To sew several beads or sequins in a row with the same length of thread, reverse stitch a seam.

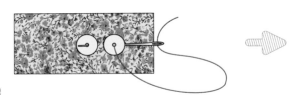

Cross-stitch

This stitch, done by hand, is a decorative stitch. It is not used for assembly, unlike the other stitches explained on pages 24 and 25. It is generally done with embroidery thread, which is thicker than sewing thread.

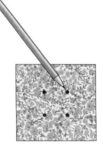

1. Mark out four points in a square on the fabric. Prepare a length of thread with a knot at the end.

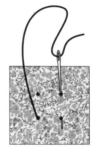

2. Pull the needle up through the bottom left point and insert it at the top right point. Come back up through the bottom right point.

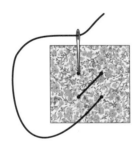

3. Push the needle back down through the last point.

4. Your cross is complete. You can make a second one on top of the first to make it more visible. Anchor the thread by making several stitches on top of one another on the back of the fabric.

Making pompoms

═══ Round pompom ═══

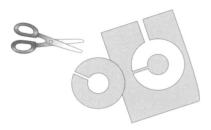

1. Cut out two cardboard circles (cereal box type) of the same size. Cut out a smaller circle and a slit in the center of each one. You can also use a plastic pompom device, sold in fabric stores.

2. Superimpose the cardboard rings, lining up the slits.
Wind the yarn around them so as to fill in the center.

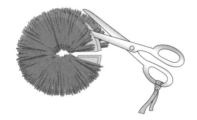

3. Cut the yarn by passing the scissors between the rings.

4. Surround the strands with another piece of yarn passed between the cardboard rings and make a knot, tightening it well.

50

5. Remove the rings and even out the pompom. Do not cut the yarn used to close the pompom—you may use it to sew the pompom to something else.

˗ˎˏ Long pompom ˎˎˏ˗

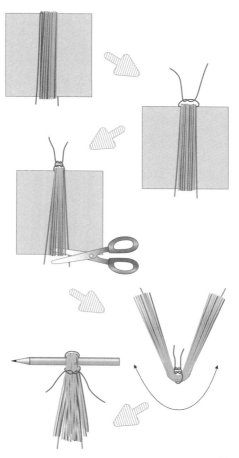

1. Take a cardboard rectangle or other object such as a book, notebook, or even your fingers. Wind yarn twenty times around the cardboard.

2. Take a strand of yarn 8 in. (20 cm) long and slip it between the cardboard and the yarn circles. Make a double knot and tighten it well.

3. On the other side, slide the scissors between the cardboard and the yarn strands.

4. Cut the threads at the bottom of the cardboard and remove it. Fold the yarns in the other direction to hide the knot.

5. Slide a pencil under this knot. Just below the pencil, to close the pompom, wind an 8-in. (20-cm) length of yarn around several times, tightening it well, and make a double knot. With the scissors, even out the threads.

Projects

Customized jeans

No need for a machine to customize a basic piece of clothing by applying fabric patterns. Who wants an original wardrobe?

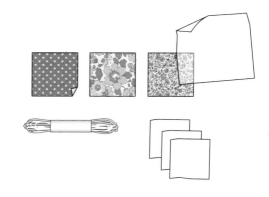

You will need:

- 3 pieces of cotton fabric measuring 5 X 5 in. (13 x 13 cm) with very small patterns (Liberty or close)
- 3 pieces of heat-activated interfacing with the same dimensions as the fabrics
- pearl cotton embroidery thread (white, or the dominant color of the fabrics, or the color of the top stitching of the jeans)
- paper (1 19½ in. x 4 in. [50 x 10 cm] strip + 2 A4 sheets [8.3 x 11.7 in.])

Other materials:

a white pencil and a black grease pencil, a ruler, a square, sewing threads matching the fabrics, a sewing needle, an embroidery needle, shears, pins, parchment paper (for cooking), an iron

★ **Dimensions of the fabric stars**
About 2¾ x 2¾ in. (7 x 7 cm) and 4 x 4 in. (10 x 10 cm)

SEE THE INTRODUCTION

COPYING A PATTERN, PAGES 18 AND 20 / PINNING, PAGE 36 / BASTING, PAGE 37 / HEMSTITCH, PAGE 25 / RUNNING STITCH, PAGE 24

Embroider the shooting star

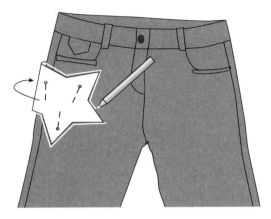

1

Copy the shooting star pattern, page 230, onto a sheet of paper and cut it out. Lay the jeans out completely flat and pin the shooting star pattern to the jeans fabric, letting part of it go around to the back. Draw the outline with the white pencil.

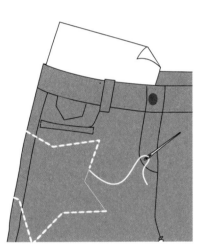

2

Remove the pattern. With a 16 in. (40 cm) long piece of white embroidery thread, embroider the outline using a running stitch. Make stitches about ¼ in. (7 mm) long, spaced about ⅛ in. (3 mm) apart. Slip a sheet of paper into the jeans, under the pattern you are embroidering, so that you do not catch the other side of the jeans with the needle.

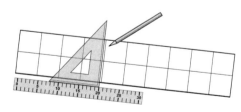

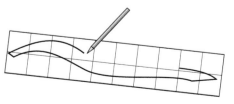

3

Prepare the pattern for the tail of the shooting star on the strip of paper: first copy the grid with the ruler and the square; then draw the pattern in the grid, square by square.

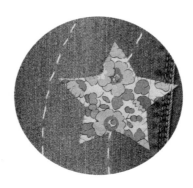

4

Cut out the pattern and pin it on the leg of the jeans, below the star you just embroidered. Trace both sides of the tail using the white pencil.

5

As for the star, embroider each side of the tail with a 19 ½ in. (50 cm) length of thread. Move the sheet of paper inside the pant leg as you embroider. If your thread gets too short, connect another piece on the back side of the pants by knotting the old thread and the new one with a very tight double knot.

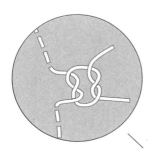

TIE OFF THE THREAD ON THE BACK.

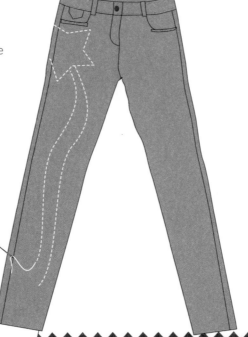

Preparing the fabrics for appliqués

6

Cut out an interfacing square so
that it is slightly smaller than one of the fabric
squares. Place the interfacing on the back side
of the fabric: the adhesive side of the
interfacing (the rougher or shinier side) must
be against the fabric.

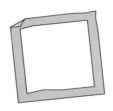

7

Place a piece of parchment paper over the
project. Taking care not to burn yourself,
set the iron to the temperature
indicated for the fabric (cotton without steam).
Place the iron on the parchment paper for a few
seconds. Remove the parchment paper
and let the fabric cool. Check that the interfacing
has adhered to the fabric. If not, iron again.

Cut out the stars

8

Copy the patterns for the stars on paper and cut
them out. Place one of the patterns on one of
the prepared fabrics, on the interfacing side.
Draw the outline in pencil.

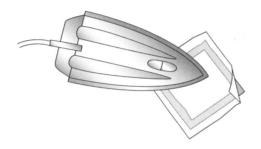

9

Cut out the interfaced fabric,
following the outline. Prepare a star in
this way on each piece of fabric
(two large and one small).

Sew the stars

10

Pin the three stars on the jeans, on top of the embroidered tail of the shooting star. Try on the jeans to see if you like the effect, taking care not to get stuck by the pins. Avoid placing a star on the knee—it may cause problems with the crease.

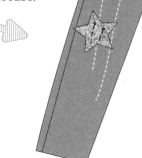

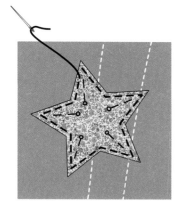

11

Lay the jeans flat again. Slip a sheet of paper into the leg, underneath each star. Baste the stars about ¾₆ in. (5 mm) from the edges.

12

Sew the stars using a hemstitch, with a matching color. Make stitches perpendicular to the edges of each star, ⅛ in. (3 mm) long, spaced apart by about ³⁄₁₆ in. (5 mm). In the hollow areas of the stars, make two stitches; on the tips, make three stitches. Remove the basting thread.

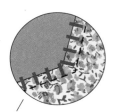

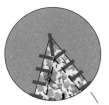

2 STITCHES IN THE HOLLOW AREAS

3 STITCHES ON THE TIPS

Yo-yo badges

These badges can be made by hand in the blink of an eye
with fabric scraps and buttons!

You will need:

- matching fabric squares measuring 4 to 6 in.
  (10 to 15 cm) per side
- round objects with a diameter of 2 ¾ in., 3 ⅛ in., and
  4 ¾ in. (7 cm, 8 cm and 12 cm) (glass, mug and small
  bowl, for example)
- buttons with a maximum diameter of ⅝ in. and ¾
  in. (1.5 and 2 cm)
- small pin holders or safety pins

Other materials:

a pencil, shears, pins, a sewing needle, thread
matching the fabrics

★ **Dimensions of the yo-yos**
about 1 ⅛ in., 1 ½ in., and 2 ⅜ in.
(3 cm, 4 cm and 6 cm) in diameter

 SEE THE INTRODUCTION

RUNNING STITCH, PAGE 24 / MAKING GATHERS, PAGE 41 / SEWING A BUTTON, PAGE 46 / FRONT TO FRONT,
PAGE 36

Cut out the fabrics

1

Use the pencil to draw a circle on the fabric, using the container of your choice for help. The finished yo-yo will be half the size of the starting diameter. Take this into account.

2

Cut along the outline. Prepare as many circles as you would like to have yo-yos.

Form the yo-yos

3

Make a double knot 4 in. (10 cm) from the end of a 12 in. (30 cm) length of thread and insert it ³⁄₁₆ in. (5 mm) from the edge of the fabric circle (on the front side).

4

Make a seam using a running stitch over the entire perimeter. The smaller the stitches are, the prettier the gathers will be! Try to stay ³⁄₁₆ in. (5 mm) from the edge at all times.

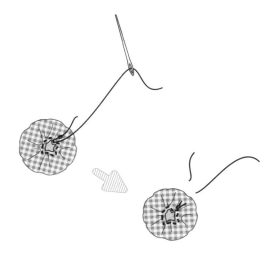

5

Pull on the thread to gather as much as possible. The circle will tighten toward the center. Flatten the yo-yo thus formed.

6

Knot both ends of the thread and cut them to ³⁄₁₆ in. (5 mm.)

Assemble the badges

7

To make a single badge, sew a button at the center of the yo-yo to cover up the gathers and hide the hole and the knot.

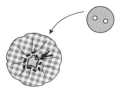

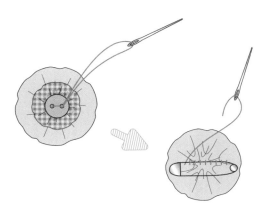

8

To make a double badge, first sew the button at the center of a small yo-yo, then sew the whole thing on a larger yo-yo.

9

Sew a pin holder or a safety pin to the back of the badge.

Flower blossoms

These voluminous flowers are made by hand
with fabric scraps. Turn one into a necklace, a key chain,
or even a pin cushion!

You will need:

For the necklace
- fabric scraps measuring at least 2 in. (5 cm) per side
- a round object with a diameter of 1 ½ in. (4 cm) (fruit juice or milk bottle cap, for example)
- pearl cotton embroidery thread in matching colors
- 8 buttons with a maximum diameter of ⅝ in. (1.5 cm)
- 1 27 ½ in. (70 cm) serpentine ribbon

For the key chain
- two fabric scraps measuring at least 2 ¾ in. (7 cm) per side
- a round object with a diameter of 2 ⅜ in. (6 cm) (small glass, for example)
- matching pearl cotton embroidery thread
- one button with a maximum diameter of ⅝ in. (1.5 cm)
- accessories: a key ring carabiner, a silver-plated chain 1 ½ in. (4 cm) long, small silver connecting rings, hanging charms, small jewelry clips

Other materials:

a pencil, scissors, pins, a sewing needle and thread matching the fabrics, synthetic stuffing, an embroidery needle, glue

★ **Dimensions**
Flowers for the necklace: 1 ½ in. (4 cm) in diameter
Flower for the key chain: 2 ⅛ in. (5.5 cm) in diameter

 SEE THE INTRODUCTION

PIN, PAGE 36 / REVERSE STITCH, PAGE 24 / OVERCAST STITCH, PAGE 25 /
NOTCHING, PAGE 39 / SEWING A BUTTON, PAGE 46 / FRONT TO FRONT, PAGE 36

Sew the fabric

1

On the back side of one of the fabric squares, use the pencil to trace a circle.

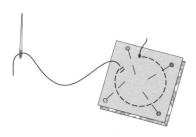

2

Pin the fabric square on another one, front to front.

3

Sew the two squares along the outline, using a reverse stitch. Make the smallest stitches possible (about ¹⁄₁₆ or ⅛ in. [2 or 3 mm]). Anchor the seam, leaving a ¾ in. (2 cm) opening so you can turn the fabric right-side out. Remove the pins and cut the ends of the thread to ⅛ in. (3 mm).

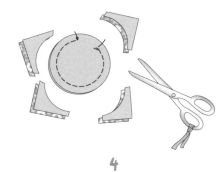

4

Cut the fabric ⅜ in. (1 cm) from the circle.

5

Notch the margin all the way around, roughly every centimeter.

Fill the flower

6

Pull the inside through the opening and turn the assembled piece right-side out.

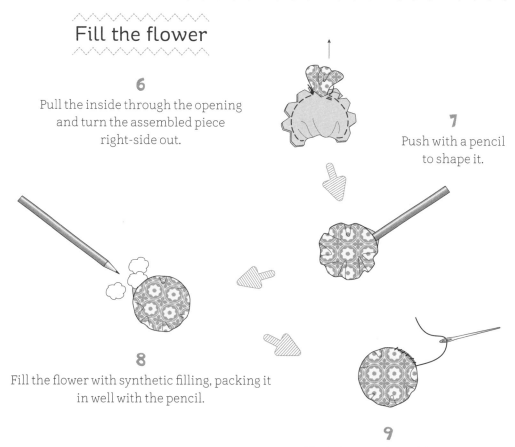

7

Push with a pencil to shape it.

8

Fill the flower with synthetic filling, packing it in well with the pencil.

9

Close the opening with a seam using an overcast stitch.

Embroider the petals

10

Thread the embroidery needle with 19 ½ in. (50 cm) of embroidery thread and make a knot 2 in. (5 cm) from the end. Insert the needle at the center of the project and pull it through to the other side.

11

Pass behind and stick the needle
in the same place to make a loop.
Pull to create a tuck.

12

Make a second stitch across from the first
in the same way. Pull firmly.

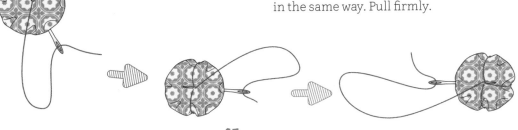

13

Always inserting the needle in the center, make two more stitches
between the first two to divide the circle in four.
Tighten the thread firmly each time.

14

Make four more stitches
between the first four
to obtain eight petals.

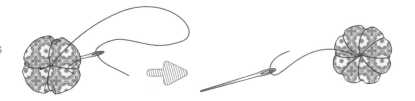

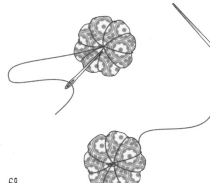

15

Insert the needle in the center, offsetting it slightly
relative to the exit point of the thread to avoid undoing
the last tuck. Pull the needle out, on the back, next to the
knot. Make a new small stitch straddling the center to
hollow it out.

16

Make two final stitches
to sew on the button.

17

On the back, make a triple knot with both ends
of the thread and cut them.
Place a dot of glue.

Necklace

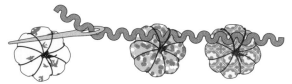

Make eight flowers 1 ½ in. (4 cm) in diameter.
With a large needle or an embroidery needle,
slide the serpentine ribbon under two stitches,
on the back of each flower.

Key chain

Make a flower with a diameter of 2 ⅜ in. (6 cm).
Slide the small chain under a stitch of the
flower, attach both of its ends in a small ring,
then connect the latter in the ring of the key
chain. Attach the charms
to the key chain with small rings.

Butterfly knots

These butterfly knots can be made very quickly,
by hand or with the machine. Barrette, purse or skirt decoration, pin...
It's up to you to decide what to do with them!

You will need:

- fabric strips measuring about 6 x 19 ½ in. (15 x 50 cm)
- for the fastener: barrette, pin holder or safety pin of an appropriate length

Other materials:

a pencil, a 12 in. (30 cm) ruler and a square, thread, a sewing machine or a needle, shears, pins, a safety pin

★ Dimensions
Large knot: 4 ¾ x 2 ⅜ in. (12 x 6 cm)
Medium knot: 4 x 2 in. (10 x 5 cm)
Small knot: 3 ⅛ x 1 ½ in. (8 x 4 cm)

SEE THE INTRODUCTION

DRAWING ON FABRIC, PAGE 20 / PINNING, PAGE 36 / STRAIGHT STITCH, PAGE 30 / REVERSE STITCH,
PAGE 24 / FRONT TO FRONT, PAGE 36 / FLATTENING SEAMS, PAGE 38 / TURNING A TUBE RIGHT-SIDE OUT, PAGE 44

Prepare the pieces of fabric

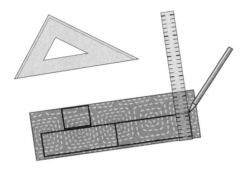

1

On the fabric, draw three rectangles,
depending on the size of the knot you wish to make.

LARGE KNOT:

2 rectangles measuring 9 ¾ x 3 ⅛ in. (25 x 8 cm)
and one rectangle measuring 2 ¾ x 3 ½ in. (7 x 9 cm)

MEDIUM KNOT:

2 rectangles measuring 8 ¾ x 2 ¾ in. (22 x 7 cm)
and one rectangle measuring 2 ⅜ x 3 ⅛ in. (6 x 8 cm)

SMALL KNOT:

2 rectangles measuring 7 x 2 ⅜ in. (18 x 6 cm)
and one rectangle measuring 2 x 2 ⅜ in. (5 x 6 cm)

Trick

IF YOUR FABRIC HAS VERY
LARGE PATTERNS, THINK ABOUT THE
AREA YOU WANT TO USE WHEN YOU CUT
IT. IF THE FABRIC HAS A GEOMETRIC
PATTERN OR LINES, TAKE THAT INTO
ACCOUNT AS WELL.

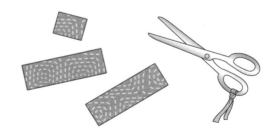

2

Cut out the rectangles.

Sew the fabric rectangles

3

Superimpose the two large rectangles, front to front. Pin them, then sew, using a straight stitch (on the machine) or reverse stitch (by hand), the long sides ⅜ in. (1 cm) from the edge. You will end up with a tube.

4

Fold the small rectangle in half, carefully superimposing its large sides, and sew ⅜ in. (1 cm) from the edge.
You will end up with another tube.

5

Flatten the seam of the small tube with your fingernail and shift it to place it in the middle.

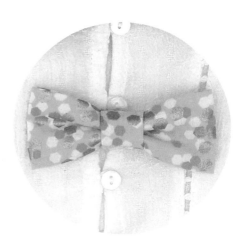

Turn the tubes right-side out

6

Following the explanations on pages 44 and 45, turn the pieces of your project right-side out so the front side of the fabric is showing.

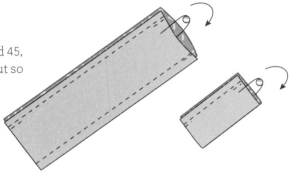

Form rings

7

Fold the two tubes in half and sew them ⅜ in. (1 cm) from the edge.

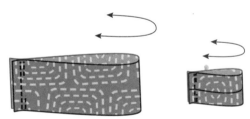

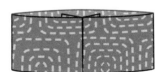

8

Turn the rings right-side out to hide the seams on the inside. Shift the seams to the center and flatten them with your fingernail.

Form the butterfly knot

9

Place the pieces, putting their seam against the table. Fold the large tube in half lengthwise.

10

Fold the sides toward the outside.

11

Fold the end of the large piece into an accordion and slide it into the small ring, toward the center. The seam of the large ring is hidden in the small ring. If necessary, turn the small ring to place the seam underneath.

12

Slip a barrette or safety pin into the small ring.

Trick

YOU CAN MAKE A FEW STITCHES BY HAND TO KEEP ALL OF THE PARTS TOGETHER.

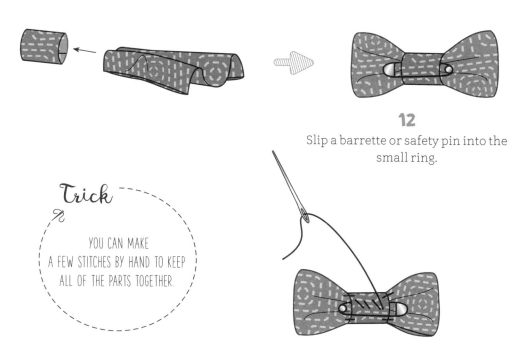

Scrunchies

A simple fabric strip and some elastic are all you need to make scrunchies, by hand or with the machine.

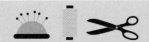

You will need:

- a fabric strip measuring 19 ½ x 4 ¾ in. (50 x 12 cm)
- 7 in. (18 cm) of flat flexible elastic measuring ⅜ in. (1 cm) wide

Other materials:

a sewing machine or a sewing needle, thread that matches the fabric, 2 safety pins

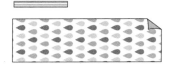

★ **Dimensions**
About 2 in. (5 cm) wide and 5 ½ in. (14 cm) in diameter

SEE THE INTRODUCTION

PINNING, PAGE 36 / STRAIGHT STITCH, PAGE 30 / REVERSE STITCH, PAGE 24 / OVERCAST STITCH, PAGE 25 / ZIGZAG STITCH, PAGE 30 / BACKSTITCHES, PAGE 31 / FRONT TO FRONT, PAGE 36

Sew the tube

1

Fold the fabric strip in half lengthwise, front to front. Place pins ¾ in. (2 cm) from the edge, along the entire length.

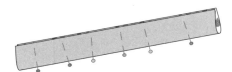

2

Sew the long side ⅜ in. (1 cm) from the edge, using a straight stitch (on the machine) or reverse stitch (by hand), leaving an opening of 2 in. (5 cm). Do not place the opening in the middle (it will be harder to turn your project right-side out later), and anchor your seams well.

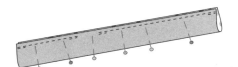

Fold the tube in half from the inside

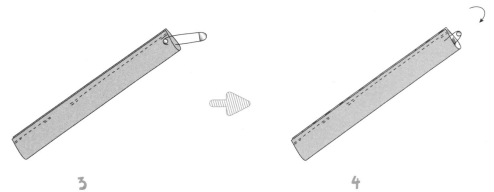

3

Remove the pins. Stick a safety pin in the end of the tube.

4

Push the safety pin into the tube and push it through the interior.

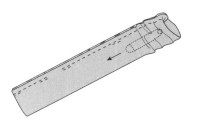

5

The fabric will crease. Pull it gently while continuing to push the pin inside.

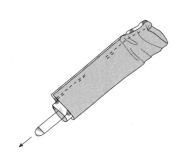

6

In this way, push the end of the tube inside itself to the halfway point, being careful not to twist it.

Sew the ends

7

Remove the safety pin. Sew the two ends of the tube together. To sew them with the machine, put the hinged presser foot in the tube and turn it as you go. Superimpose the beginning and end of the seam carefully. If this is too delicate, sew by hand using a reverse stitch.

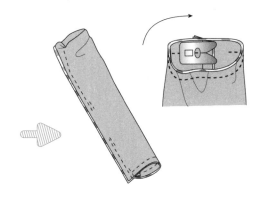

Turn the scrunchie right-side out

8

Take the tube out through the opening to turn it right-side out: you have a ring!

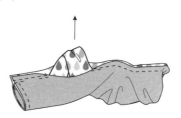

9

Iron the ring now, because later it will be gathered and ironing will no longer be possible.

Insert the elastic

10

Stick a safety pin in each end of the elastic. Put the first end of the elastic in the tube through the opening. The second pin will allow the second end of the elastic to remain outside.

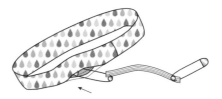

11

Go all the way around the ring with the elastic. When the safety pin passes by the seam, it may become stuck in the folds of the fabric: move the sides of the ring away slightly to allow it to pass.

12

Superimpose ¾ in. or 1 ⅛ in. (2 or 3 cm) of the two ends of the elastic. Sew them by hand by making a large number of stitches, before removing the safety pins. You can also sew them with the machine with a few tight zigzag stitches in both directions. In this case, baste by hand first.

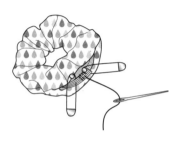 

13

Close the opening of the scrunchie using an overcast stitch.

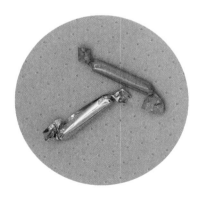 

Bandannas

Making a bandanna will teach you to make hems and use the zigzag stitch on the sewing machine. If you have more experience, you can even decorate your scarf with an appliqué heart and sequins.

You will need:

- a fabric square measuring 27 ½ in. (70 cm) per side, preferably reversible: to cut it while following a straight line, follow the first steps of the explanations
- a fabric square measuring 4 in. (10 cm) per side for the heart
- 14 sequins with a diameter of ¼ in. (6–7 mm)

Other materials:

a pencil, a tape measure, sewing thread in contrasting colors, a sewing machine, shears, pins, paper, tracing paper, a grease pencil

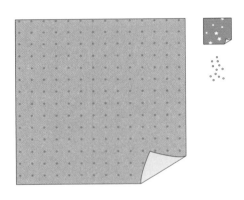

★ Dimensions
25 x 25 in. (64 x 64 cm)

SEE THE INTRODUCTION

DRAWING ON FABRIC, PAGE 20 / PINNING, PAGE 36 / BASTING, PAGE 37 / IRONING, PAGE 12 / MAKING A HEM, PAGE 40 / ZIGZAG STITCHES, PAGE 30 / BACKSTITCHING, PAGE 31 / COPYING A PATTERN, PAGES 18 AND 20 / SEWING SEQUINS, PAGE 48 / SELVAGE, PAGE 15 / FIBER DIRECTION, PAGE 15

Cut out the square

1

The more you respect the direction of the fiber, the easier it will be to fold the hems. Place the selvage facing you. Spread the tape measure out along the selvage and draw two reference marks 27 ½ in. (70 cm) apart. Draw a line between the two reference marks.

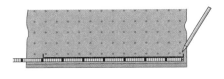

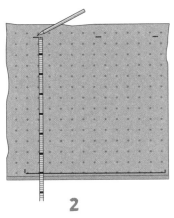

2

Mark three reference marks 27 ½ in. (70 cm) above this line, 8 in. (20 cm) apart.

3

Draw a line that passes through these reference marks.

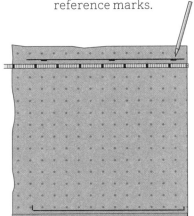

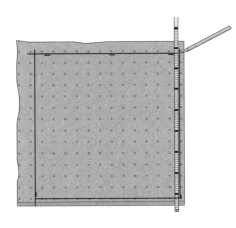

4

Draw two perpendicular lines that start from the bottom reference marks and follow the direction of the thread. Your square is drawn. Cut it by following the outlines.

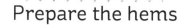

5

On the back side, make a ⅝ in. (1.5 cm) hem on one side: to do so, fold the fabric twice over ⅝ in. (1.5 cm). Baste the hem. Make another hem on the opposite edge and baste it.

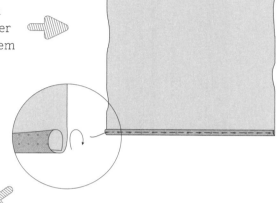

6

Fold the other two sides in the same way. The hems are superimposed in the corners.

7

If the fabric is thin enough, fold the ends of the last hems toward the inside before basting them.

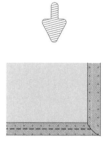

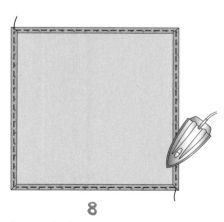

8

Flatten the hems with the iron.

Conduct sewing tests

9

On a scrap of fabric folded in three, make zigzag stitches with different lengths and widths. Sew at least 4 in. (10 cm) as a test. Try to turn a corner to see what happens. Note any lengths and widths used so that you will remember them.

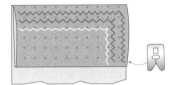

Sew the hem

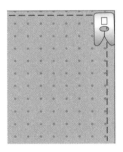 

10

Choose the first stitch and a thread color. The sewing is done on the front side of the fabric. Start sewing the hems in one corner by aligning your presser foot along the edge of the fabric. Make backstitches (tight zigzag) to start and sew the first side, stopping about ¾ in. (2 cm) from the following corner.

11

Complete the seam by turning the hand wheel so you do not go too far, or too fast. Anchor the seam about ⅜ in. (1 cm) before the edge.

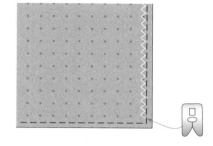

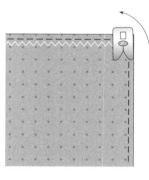

12

Raise the presser foot, leaving the needle in the fabric, and rotate the fabric.
Lower the presser foot so that it is aligned against the edge of the second side.

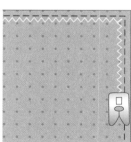

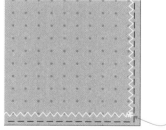

13

Continue the seam.
Sew the entire perimeter of the bandanna in this way.

14

At the end, make several backstitches.
Remove the basting.

Create a decorative border

15

You can make several parallel seams with different colors and stitches.

 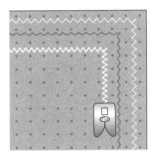

To do this, start with the one closest to the edge and align the presser foot against it to do the next one. In this case, you will not only sew on the hem, but also on a single layer of the fabric. Do some test runs beforehand. If the fabric is thin, the stitches may crease.

Prepare the heart appliqué

16

Copy the pattern for the heart, page 231, onto the paper and cut it out. Trace the outline with the pencil on the fabric.

17

Cut out the fabric, following the outline.

18

Fold the bandanna in four and pin the heart on one quarter of the bandanna, pointing the tip toward the corner. Take care to pin only one layer of the bandanna. Unfold the bandanna.

Sew the heart

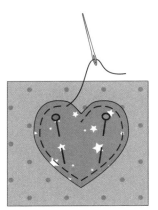

19

Baste the heart ³⁄₁₆ in. (5 mm) from the edge.

20

Remove the pins. Sew the heart using the machine with a contrasting thread, using a zigzag stitch with a medium width and length. To do this, start the seam at the indentation of the heart and make a few backstitches.

Sew very slowly, aligning the middle of the presser foot on the edge of the heart and raising it from time to time (with the needle embedded in the fabric) to turn. Go all the way around the heart and finish with a few stitches in place. Remove the basting thread.

Make the sequined arrow

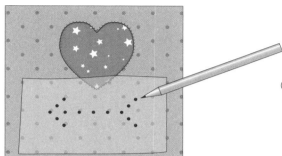

21

Copy the pattern for the arrow, page 231, under the heart onto the tracing paper.

22

With a 19 ½ in. (50 cm) length of matching thread, sew the sequins in a row, as explained on page 48, following the order of the diagrams.

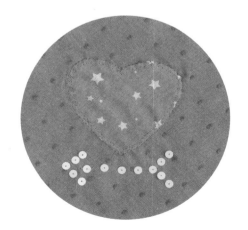

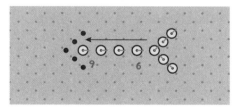

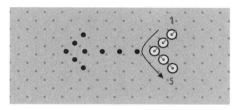

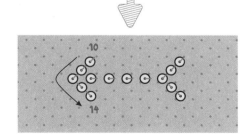

Triangle scarf with braid

With this project, you will learn to cut fabric on the bias and to sew the zigzag stitch on the machine. For perfect finishing touches, use different color threads on top and on bottom.

You will need:

- 16 in. (40 cm) of a fabric sold in a 59 in. (150 cm) width (a light fabric, preferably reversible)
- 3 ¾ yards (3.5 m) of matching braid
- for the pompoms: yarn, a pompom device with a diameter of 1 ½ in. (4 cm) or two pieces of cardboard measuring 4 in. (10 cm) per side

Other materials:

a pencil, a tape measure, thread in the two dominant colors (background of the fabric and braid) of the same quality and same brand, a sewing machine, shears, pins

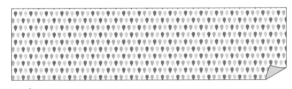

★ **Dimensions**
59 in. (150 cm) wide and 16 in. (40 cm) long

SEE THE INTRODUCTION

BASTING, PAGE 37 / MAKING A HEM, PAGE 40 / ZIGZAG STITCH, PAGE 30 / BACKSTITCHING, PAGE 31 / MAKING POMPOMS, PAGE 50 / FRONT TO FRONT, PAGE 36 / FLATTENING SEAMS, PAGE 38 / BIAS OF THE FABRIC, PAGE 15

Cut the fabric

1

If necessary, cut the fabric cleanly along one of the large sides, so that it is perfectly straight. If the second large side is not as clean, this is not a problem. Fold the fabric in half widthwise, front to front, aligning the edges well. Pin the small sides. Position the clean edge toward you.

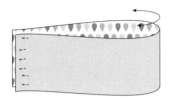

2

With the tape measure, draw a diagonal line starting from the top of the crease, up to ¾ in. (2 cm) above the tip. If the line is difficult to draw, instead draw reference marks every 4 in. (10 cm).

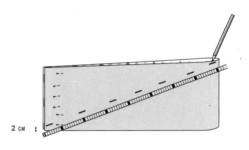

2 CM

3

Pin the two layers of fabric, placing the pins below the reference marks.

4

Cut the two layers of fabric, following the reference marks.

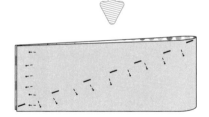

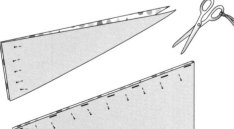

5

Unfold the fabric.
You will have a triangle with slightly overlapping tips on both sides.

Baste the hems

6

Place the triangle with the back side facing you and start with the longest length, on the right. Fold the fabric as you sew: over a length of 4 in. (10 cm), make the narrowest possible fold (³⁄₁₆ in. or 5 mm), then a second fold the same height. Crush them with your fingernail.

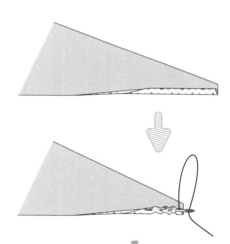

7

Sew the basting thread.

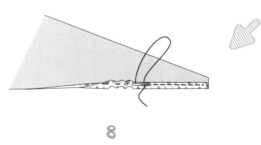

8

Do the same thing for the next 4 in. (10 cm). Continue in the same manner over the entire length of the fabric. Do not pull too much, so as to avoid puckering the fabric.

Trick

YOU WILL NEED TO CHANGE THREAD DURING THE BASTING. MAKE A FEW STITCHES ON TOP OF ONE ANOTHER TO ANCHOR THREAD THAT HAS BECOME TOO SHORT, THEN CONTINUE WITH A NEW LENGTH OF THREAD.

9

Fold twice at the end, then fold the beginning of the next side. Make a stitch to hold the tip.

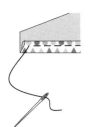  

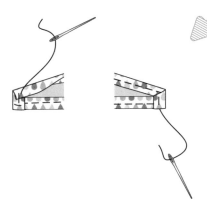

10

Baste the hem on the other two sides on the bias in the same way. The fabric will be more elastic on these sides, and the hem will be more delicate to fold. Crush it well with your fingernail. Fold the second tip like the first before finishing the basting on the last side.

Baste the braid

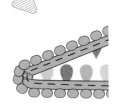

11

Place the end of the braid on the front side, in the middle of the long side, letting the small pompoms hang off, then baste the braid along the long side as you go.

12

Go all the way around the triangular scarf, bending the braid around the corners.

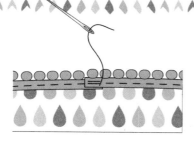

13

When you finish going around, cut the braid, leaving a ¾ in. (2 cm) tail. Superimpose the two ends, and make a stitch to assemble them firmly.

Stitch everything using the machine

14

Prepare the machine using thread the color of the braid for the spool and thread matching the fabric for the bobbin. Do a few tests with the zigzag stitch by sewing a scrap of braid onto a scrap of fabric to adjust the width: the zigzag must not be wider than the braid.

15

Pierce the braid with the zigzag stitch, starting at the connection. Begin and end with backstitches, which prevent the ends of the braid from fraying.

Finishing touches

16

Remove the basting threads from the hem and the braid. Make two pompoms. Sew the pompoms to the two tips by passing the thread through the center.

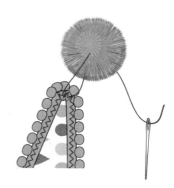

Striped scarf

Fairly easy to make, this scarf is perfect for learning
to sew straight on the machine! Have fun mixing fabric prints.
If you are comfortable, sew directly on the pins, without basting!

You will need:

- coordinated fabric strips measuring 19 ½ in. (50 cm)
wide (12 strips for the photographed model): two
13 ¾ in. (35 cm) strips, three 7 in. (18 cm) strips, two
6 in. (15 cm) strips, five 4 in. (10 cm) strips

Other materials:

a pencil, a tape measure, thread (white or ecru if
the dominant color of the fabrics is light, black if
the dominant color is dark), a sewing machine,
a needle, shears, pins, an iron

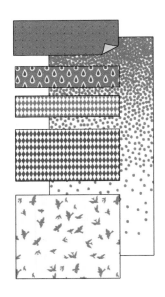

★ **Dimensions**
About 9 ½ in. (24 cm) wide
and 5 feet 10 ¾ in. (1.80 m) long

SEE THE INTRODUCTION

DRAWING ON FABRIC, PAGE 20 / PINNING, PAGE 36 / BASTING, PAGE 37 / STRAIGHT STITCH, PAGE 30 /
OVERCAST STITCH, PAGE 25 / FRONT TO FRONT, PAGE 36 / FLATTENING SEAMS, PAGE 38 / NOTCHING, PAGE 39

Position the fabrics

1

On a large table or a clean floor, position the strips below one another, alternating the patterns and heights until you find an order you like.

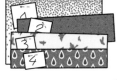

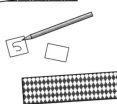

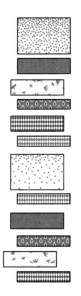

2

So that you can remember the order you decided on, number the strips by pinning pieces of paper on them, or place them on top of one another in order. You can also take a picture before you pick up the strips.

Assemble the strips

3

Assemble the first two strips, front to front, by the long side, placing the pins perpendicularly, ¾ in. (2 cm) from the edge.

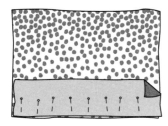

4

Make a seam ⅜ in. (1 cm) from the edge.

5

Unfold the strips.

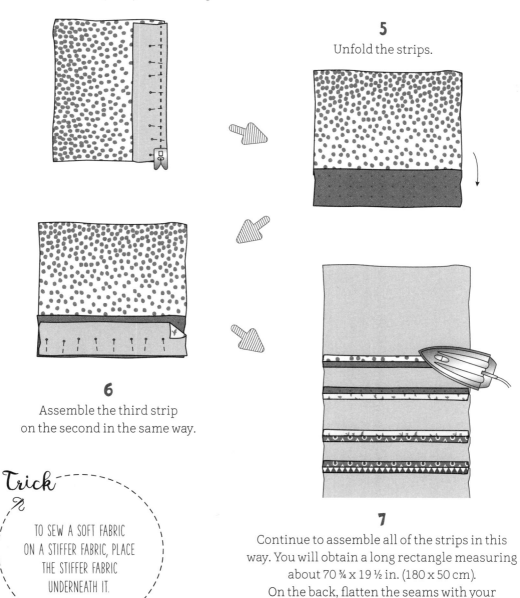

6

Assemble the third strip
on the second in the same way.

Trick

TO SEW A SOFT FABRIC
ON A STIFFER FABRIC, PLACE
THE STIFFER FABRIC
UNDERNEATH IT.

7

Continue to assemble all of the strips in this
way. You will obtain a long rectangle measuring
about 70 ¾ x 19 ½ in. (180 x 50 cm).
On the back, flatten the seams with your
fingernail, then with an iron.

Sew the scarf

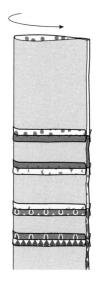

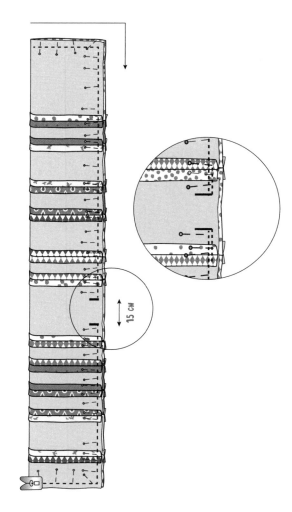

8

Fold the rectangle in half lengthwise, front to front, aligning the edges carefully and placing the seams across from each other.

9

Pin all three sides.
Make sure to place pins on all of the folds of the seams to hold them well.
Around the middle of the long side, draw two pencil lines about 6 in. (15 cm) apart: place them in the middle of a fairly wide strip of fabric, and not on the seams.

10

Sew all three sides ⅜ in. (1 cm) from the edge, anchoring the seam at the pencil marks to leave an opening. Make backstitches at the beginning and end of the seam, and on either side of the opening.

15 CM

11

Notch the four corners and remove all of the pins.

12

Pull the scarf through the opening to turn it right-side out.

13

Push into the corners with a pencil.

14

Close the opening by sewing by hand, using an overcast stitch. Iron the scarf.

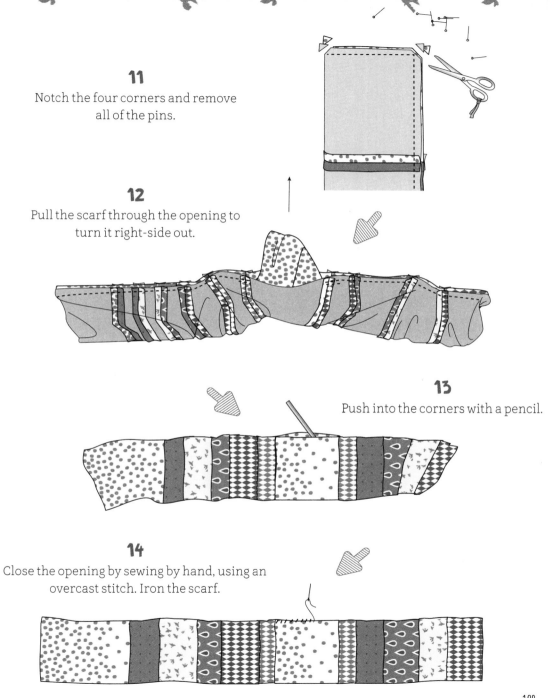

Headbands

With three widths to choose from, these headbands are easy to make.
You can make a few and wear them together
or separately!

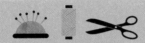

You will need:

- a strip of fabric 17 ¼ in. (44 cm) long and, depending on the selected width of the headband:
2 ⅜ in. (6 cm) (skinny headband), 4 ¼ in. (11 cm) (medium headband) or 6 ¼ in. (16 cm) (wide headband) wide
- a strip of matching fabric 8 in. (20 cm) long and 2 ⅜ in. (6 cm) (skinny headband), 3 ½ in. (9 cm) (medium headband) or 4 ¼ in. (11 cm) (wide headband) wide
- 4 in. (10cm) of flat flexible elastic measuring ¾ in. (2 cm) wide

Other materials:

a sewing machine, thread that matches the fabrics, pins, shears, 2 safety pins, an iron

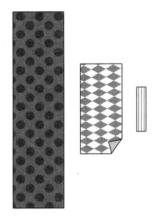

★ Size
54 to 56, adjustable depending on the head size

SEE THE INTRODUCTION

PINNING, PAGE 36 / IRONING, PAGE 12 / BASTING, PAGE 37 / STRAIGHT STITCH, PAGE 30 /
BACKSTITCHES, PAGE 31 / FRONT TO FRONT, PAGE 36 / TURNING A TUBE RIGHT-SIDE OUT, PAGE 44

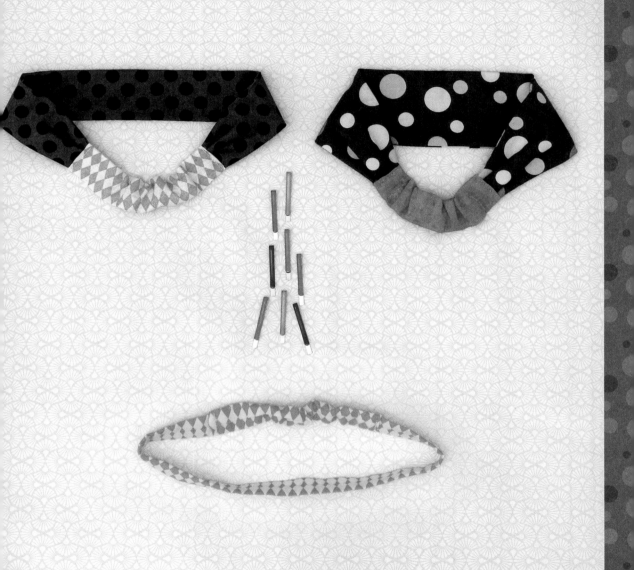

Sew the tubes

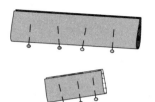

1

Fold the two strips of fabric in half lengthwise, front to front.
Place pins ¾ in. (2 cm) from the edge, across the entire length.

2

Sew the edge of each strip together using a straight stitch on the machine, ⅜ in. (1 cm) from the edge of the open long side, starting and ending with backstitches.

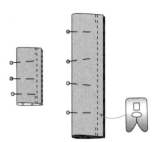

Turn the tubes right-side out

3

Following the explanations on pages 44 and 45, turn the two pieces you have just sewn right-side out.

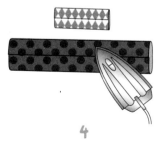

4

Shift the seam of each tube to the middle and iron them.

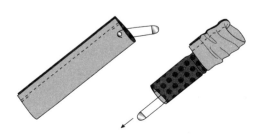

Insert the elastic into the small tube

5

Fold each end of the small tube ⅜ in. (1 cm)
toward the inside. Use a sharpened
pencil to help.

6

Stick a safety pin
on each end of the elastic
and pull the elastic into the tube.

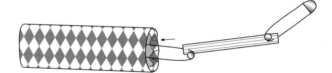

7

Take the pin out the other side. The fabric will
gather. The second pin will allow the second
end of the elastic to remain outside.

Block the elastic

8

Flatten one end of the tube and fasten the elastic with a pin. To be safe, leave the safety pin in place if it doesn't bother you when you sew. Make a stitch ¾ in. (2 cm) from the end of the tube. At the end, leave the tube on the machine, with the needle in the fabric.

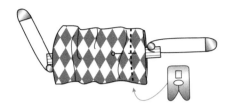

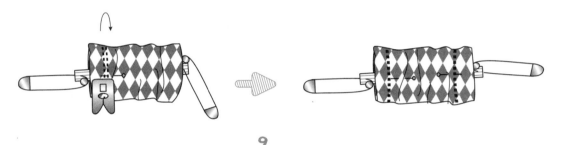

9

Raise the presser foot, turn the tube over, lower the foot again. Make a second line of stitches on top of the first one to make it more solid. Sew the other end in the same way.

Assemble the two tubes

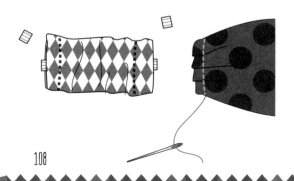

10

Remove the safety pins and straight pins, then cut the protruding ends of the elastic. If you have chosen to make a medium or wide headband, make one or two folds at one end of the wide tube to give it the same width as the small tube. Baste the folds.

11

Place the end of the large tube inside the small tube until it reaches the stitch holding the elastic in place. Baste.

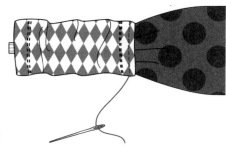

12

Make a line of stitches in both directions on the small tube, very close to the edge. If you have trouble sewing because of the thickness, run the machine by hand so it doesn't slip. Remove the basting thread.

13

Assemble the other two ends in the same way.

Bookmark

This item can be made very quickly by hand or with the machine, using fabric scraps, ribbon and yarn. Sew a few of these to customize all of your books and notebooks, or give them as gifts!

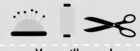

You will need:

- 2 fabric rectangles measuring 2 ¾ X 5 in. (7 x 13 cm) (small model) or 2 ¾ X 7 in. (7 x 18 cm) (large model)
- 6 in. (15 cm) of cotton ribbon or knitting yarn

Other materials:

paper, pencil, matching thread, a sewing machine (optional), a needle, shears, pins, an iron

Dimensions (without ribbon)
Small model: 1 ½ in. (4 cm) wide and 4 in. (10 cm) long
Large model: 1 ½ in. (4 cm) wide and 6 in. (15 cm) long

SEE THE INTRODUCTION

USING A PATTERN, PAGE 18 / DRAWING ON FABRIC, PAGE 20 / PINNING, PAGE 36 / STRAIGHT STITCH, PAGE 30 / BACKSTITCHING, PAGE 31 / REVERSE STITCH, PAGE 24 / NOTCHING, PAGE 39 / OVERCAST STITCH, PAGE 25 / HEMSTITCH, PAGE 25 / MAKING A HEM, PAGE 40 / LONG POMPOM, PAGE 51 / FRONT TO FRONT, PAGE 36 / IRONING, PAGE 12

Prepare the elements

1

On the front of one of the two fabric rectangles, pin the ribbon in the center carefully, letting one end protrude by ⅜ in. (1 cm) from the top. Align the pins along the ribbon without letting them go past the sides so they do not get in the way of the seam.

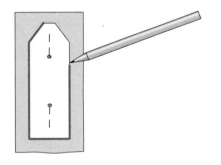

2

Draw the pattern from page 231 on the paper and cut it out. On the back of the second fabric rectangle, pin the pattern, centering it carefully. Draw its outline with the pencil.

3

Remove the pattern. Pin the rectangle with the outline on the other rectangle, front to front, aligning the tip of the shape on the end of the ribbon protruding from the top.

Make the seam

 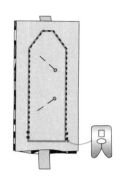

4

Sew using a straight stitch (with the machine) or a reverse stitch (by hand) on the pencil outline, leaving the side without the tip open. On the machine, begin and end the seam with backstitches, and to turn the corners, raise the presser foot, leaving the needle in the fabric.

Reduce the margins

5

Cut the fabric around the outline, ⅜ in. (1 cm) from the edge. Remove the pins.

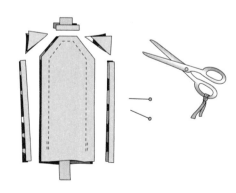

Rotate the fabric

6

Gently pull on the ribbon to turn the bookmark right-side out (remove the pins from the ribbon as you go).

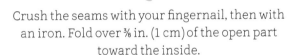

7

Push the corners with a pencil.

8

Crush the seams with your fingernail, then with an iron. Fold over ⅜ in. (1 cm) of the open part toward the inside.

9

Close the opening using an overcast stitch.

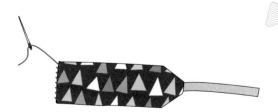

Decorate the ribbon

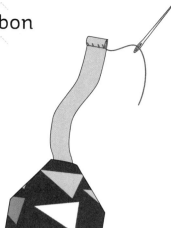

10

Fold the end of the ribbon down over ³⁄₁₆ in. (5 mm).
Fold a second time.
Sew this hem.

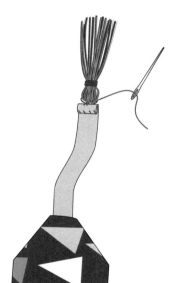

11

Make a long pompom (see page 51) by wrapping the
yarn 20 times around your fingers, and sew it to the
end of the ribbon, using a few overcast stitches.

115

String of pennants

Teach yourself to sew corners and it will be easy for you to sew lots of these pennants and make strings of any length!

You will need:

- 14 rectangles of different fabrics measuring 7 x 9 in. (18 x 23 cm) (2 per pennant)
- 4 ft. 1 ¼ in. (1.25 m) of piping

Other materials:

bristol board or light cardboard, a black grease pencil, thread to match the fabrics and piping, a sewing machine, a needle, shears, pins, a ruler, a square

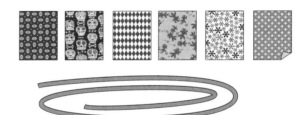

★ Dimensions
The pictured string is about 3 ft. 3 ¼ in. (1 meter) long (7 pennants). The number of pennants and the length of the piping can be adapted based on the size of the room to be decorated.

SEE THE INTRODUCTION

PINNING, PAGE 36 / BASTING, PAGE 37 / SEWING PIPING, PAGE 42 / FRONT TO FRONT, PAGE 36 / STRAIGHT STITCH, PAGE 30 / BACKSTITCH, PAGE 31

Prepare the pattern

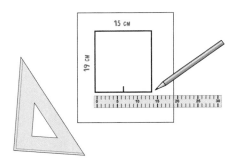

1

On the bristol board, use the ruler and square to draw a 6 x 7 ½ in. (15 x 19 cm) rectangle. Draw a reference mark in the middle of the bottom side.

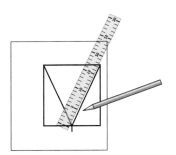

2

Next, draw two lines that start from this reference mark going up to the top corners. You will end up with a triangle. Cut it out. This shape will be your pattern to draw identical triangles on the fabric.

Start a pennant

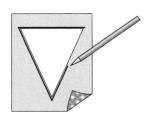

3

On the back of one of the fabric rectangles, place the pattern and draw its outline with the pencil. If the pattern of the fabric has a direction, make sure to place the tip at the bottom.

4

Pin the fabric rectangle on a second fabric rectangle, front to front, placing the pins inside the drawn triangle.

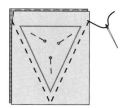

Sew the pennant

5

Baste the two long sides of the triangle outside the outline, at ³⁄₁₆ in. (5 mm).

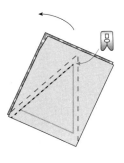

6

Remove the pins and sew along the outline.
Start the seam at the edge of the fabric, on the smallest side, and sew the first line to the tip. When the needle is in the tip of the triangle, raise the presser foot. Rotate the fabric to place the presser foot in the axis of the second line of the outline. Lower the presser foot and sew the second line to the edge.

Finish the pennant

7

Remove the basting thread.

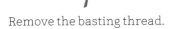

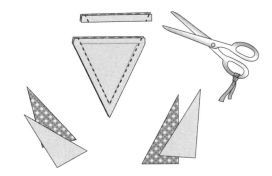

8

Cut the fabric ⅜ in. (1 cm) from the outline. The seam will also be cut, but this won't be a problem.

9

Cut the tip without touching the seam.

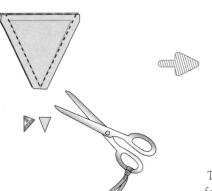

10

Turn the pennant over so the front side is facing up. Push the tip gently with a pencil.

11

Iron the pennant, being careful
not to burn yourself. Cut both of the protruding tips.

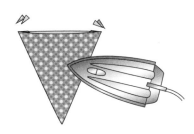

~~~~~~~~~
Sew the other pennants
~~~~~~~~~

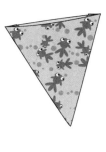

12

Make the other pennants
the same way.

Sew the piping

13

Place the pennants next to each other and pin the piping, aligning it on the edges. Leave about 4 in. (10 cm) of piping before the first pennant and after the last one.

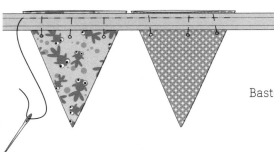

14

Baste the piping on all of the pennants in a row, on their uppermost crease.

15

Remove the pins. Use the sewing machine to stitch slightly above the crease, starting and ending with backstitches. Remove the basting thread.

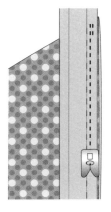

16

Fold the piping down on the back and baste it over the entire length, even in the spaces between the pennants.

17

Stitch ⅟₁₆ in. (2 mm) from the edge. Remove the basting thread.

Drawstring bags

Practical and indispensable in many situations,
here is a basic model in two sizes. Once you get the
hang of sewing this, feel free to make it in other formats.

You will need:

- 2 fabric rectangles: 9 x 12 ½ in. (23 x 32 cm) (large model) or 7 x 10 ¼ in. (18 x 26 cm) (small model)
- String or shoelace: 31 ½ in. (80 cm) minimum
- a large wooden bead (with a hole having a diameter of ⅛ or ³⁄₁₆ in. (4 or 5 mm)

Other materials:

matching thread, a sewing machine, a needle, shears, pins, a safety pin, small, pointy scissors or a seam ripper, scotch tape or clear nail polish

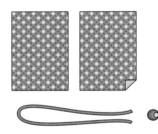

★ Dimensions
Large model: 8 in. (20 cm) wide and 10 ¼ in. (26 cm) high
Small model: 6 in. (15 cm) wide and 8 in. (20 cm) high

SEE THE INTRODUCTION

DRAWING ON FABRIC, PAGE 20 / PINNING, PAGE 36 / STRAIGHT STITCH, PAGE 30 / ZIGZAG STITCH, PAGE 30 / BACKSTITCHES, PAGE 31 / FRONT TO FRONT, PAGE 36 / NOTCHING, PAGE 39

Sew the pouch

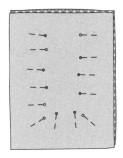

1

Pin the two fabric rectangles front to front, placing the pins ¾ in. (2 cm) from the edge. Pay attention to the direction of the pattern if necessary.

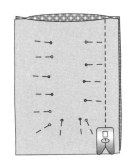

2

Sew ⅝ in. (1.5 cm) from the edge on three sides. Start by sewing the right side until you are ⅝ in. (1.5 cm) from the bottom. Leaving the needle in the fabric, raise the presser foot, rotate the fabric into the axis of the bottom side, lower the presser foot and sew the side until you are ⅝ in. (1.5 cm) from the third side. Rotate like before and sew until the end.

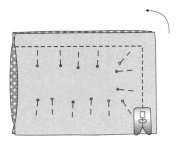

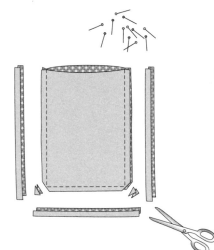

3

Remove the pins. Cut the edges to ⅜ in. (1 cm) so that they are straight and the bag is clean inside. Notch the corners at ³⁄₁₆ in. (5 mm) from the seam.

Overcast the pouch

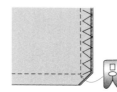

4

Overcast the first large side starting from the non-sewn edge, with the widest zigzag stitch using a medium length.
Start the seam with backstitches.

5

In the corner, raise your presser foot, leaving the needle in the fabric.

6

Rotate slightly. Lower the presser foot and overcast the corner. Raise it again, leaving the needle in the fabric.

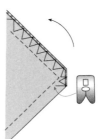

7

Rotate again and overcast the short side.

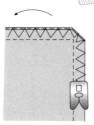

8

Overcast the second corner and the long side in the same way. Finish the seam with backstitches.

Make the casing

9

Fold down the upper edge of the pouch over ⅜ in. (1 cm), on the back side, and mark the fold with your fingernail.

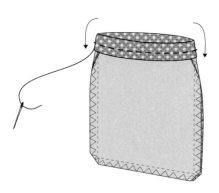

10

Make a second fold of 1 ⅛ in. (3 cm). Baste at ³⁄₁₆ in. (5 mm) from the edge of the fold.

11

Stitch with the machine just below the baste. To do this, remove the removable tray from the machine. Raise the presser foot and slip the pouch around the plate.

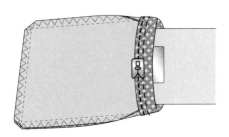

12

Turn the bag over so it is right-side up. Push the corners all the way out with a pencil.
Iron the bag, being careful not to burn yourself.

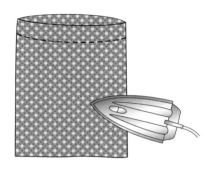

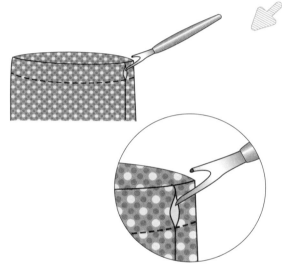

13

With the tip of a small pair of scissors or a seam ripper, cut the tips and unstitch the seam on one side, between the seam of the casing and the top of the bag.
Be very careful not to cut the fabric.

14

Stick a safety pin in each end of the string. If you use a shoelace with an end that is stiff enough, you can skip the safety pin. Slip the string into the casing by pushing on the safety pin.

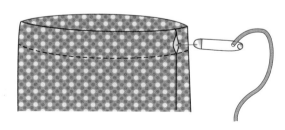

15

Go all the way around the casing. When the safety pin passes by the seam, it may become stuck in the margins of the fabric: move the sides of the casing away slightly to help it pass. Take the string out through the opening.

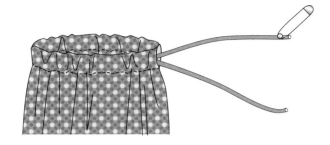

16

Slide the bead onto both ends of the shoelace or the string. To make it easier, you can stiffen the ends by winding some scotch tape around the ends or putting a bit of clear nail polish on them.

17

Make a knot at each end of the string and cut to ¾ in. (2 cm).

Variations

For a laundry bag, make two 16 x 19 ½ in. (40 x 50 cm) rectangles, and for a shoe bag, two 12 x 16 in. (30 x 40 cm) rectangles. Adapt the length of the string accordingly.

Tissue pouches

Ideal for small gifts, these pouches require few supplies, but are always useful! The only hard part will be sewing a few layers of fabric at the same time.

You will need:

- 2 rectangles of fabric in matching colors measuring 7 x 6 in. (18 x 15 cm)
- 2 ⅜ in. (6 cm) of ribbon

Other materials:

matching sewing thread, a sewing machine, a needle, shears, a ruler and a pencil

★ **Dimensions when flat**
3 in. x 5 ¼ in. (7.5 x 13 cm)

SEE THE INTRODUCTION

PINNING, PAGE 36 / BASTING, PAGE 37 / FRONT TO FRONT, PAGE 36 / STRAIGHT STITCH, PAGE 30 / ZIGZAG STITCH, PAGE 30 / BACKSTITCH, PAGE 31

Assemble the two fabrics

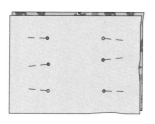

1

Place the two fabrics front to front, and pin them along the two short sides, ¾ in. (2 cm) from the edges.

2

Stitch the short sides ⅜ in. (1 cm) from the edges. Start and finish the seams with backstitches. You will end up with a tube.

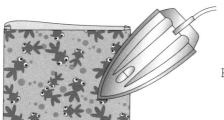

3

Pull the tube through so it is right-side out. Iron it, being careful not to burn yourself.

Form the pouch

4

With contrasting thread, make a top stitch in the zigzag stitch on both of the sides you want to sew, ⅜ in. (1 cm) from the edges. It is not necessary to anchor these top stitches at the beginning and the end.

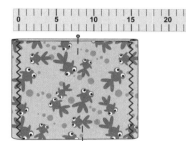

5

Choose the face that will be on the outside and place it on top. Using a ruler, find the middle and mark it with a pin on the top and bottom.

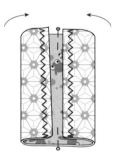

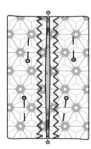

6

Fold both sides down toward the middle, bringing them together against the pins.

7

Pin the flaps.

Prepare the ribbon

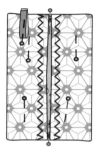

8

Fold the ribbon in half, back to back
if there is a front side, and pin it perpendicular
to the edge, in the middle of one of the folds.
The ends of the ribbon should protrude slightly.

Close the pouch

9

Baste the sides by hand a little over ⅜ in.(1 cm)
from the edge. Remove the pins.

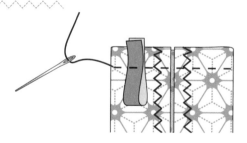

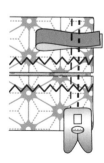

10

Sew the two sides together ⅜ in. (1 cm) from
the edge (you will sew the ribbon with them),
starting and ending with backstitches.
Remove the basting thread.

11

Cut the sides ³⁄₁₆ in. (0.5 cm) from the edges.

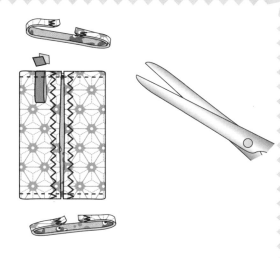

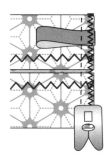

12

Overcast the edges on the zigzag stitch fairly tightly, anchoring the stitch well at the beginning and the end.

Turn the pouch

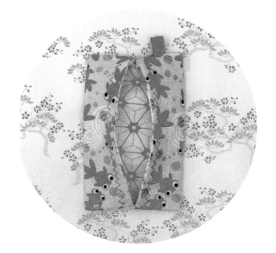

13

Turn the pouch right-side out. The ribbon will be on the outside. Push the corners of the pouch out with a pencil. All you need to do now is take the tissues out of the plastic and put them in the pouch! If you like, you can slide a key ring into the loop of ribbon.

Planner cover

This project will teach you to measure a planner
or notebook to make a customized cover that fits perfectly.
It will also teach you the basics of embroidery.

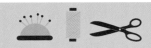

You will need:

- a planner or notebook
- denim: a rectangle large enough to cut out the cover,
  the pouch and the bookmark (patterns, page 232)
- pearl cotton embroidery thread in orange or
  another bright color

Other materials:

paper, a ruler, a square, a black pencil, a white
pencil, tracing paper, thread matching the embroidery thread, a sewing machine, an embroidery
needle, shears, pins

★ Dimensions of the planner used for the
pictured model
About 6 in. (15 cm) wide, 8 ½ in. (21.5 cm)
high and ⅜ in. (1 cm) thick

SEE THE INTRODUCTION

COPYING A PATTERN, PAGES 18 AND 20 / DRAWING ON FABRIC, PAGE 20 / PINNING, PAGE 36 / STRAIGHT STITCH,
PAGE 30 / BACKSTITCHES, PAGE 31 / REVERSE STITCH, PAGE 24 / FRONT TO FRONT, PAGE 36 / FIBER DIRECTION, PAGE 15

Preparing the cover

1

Measure the planner or notebook you want to cover.

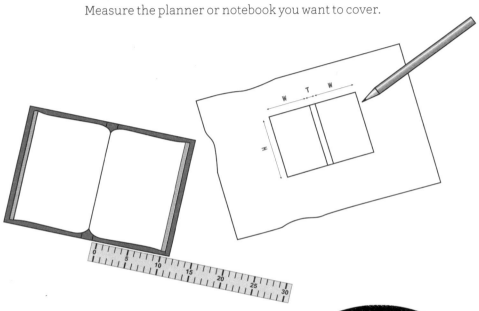

On the paper, note its width (W),
its height (H) and its thickness (T).
Round these measurements to the next highest
quarter-inch or half-centimeter (0.51 in. = ½ in.;
6.22 in. = 6 ¼ in. or 1.3 cm = 1.5 cm;
15.8 cm = 16 cm). Make a diagram
of the open cover.

2

Add 4 in. (10 cm) to each side for the flaps and ⅝ in. (1.5 cm) to the top and bottom. Add the measurements to calculate the size of the fabric rectangle to be cut.

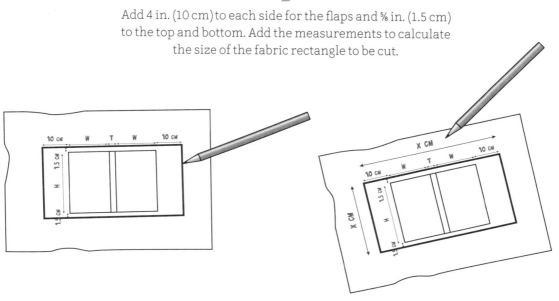

3

With the ruler and square, draw the rectangle on the denim using the white pencil. Make sure to draw the lines along the grain so that the denim doesn't fray later. Cut out the cover.

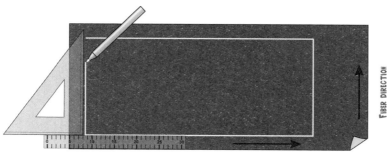

Shape the cover

4

Spread the fabric rectangle out toward you.
Place the planner open to the first page, about
4 in. (10 cm) from the left edge, and in the
middle heightwise.

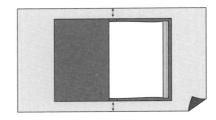

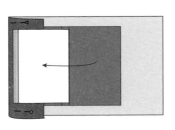

5

Fold the fabric on the left onto the cover
of the planner and pin it at the top and bottom.

6

Now open the planner to the last page.
Fold the fabric on the right onto the cover. Close the planner, then pin the flap.

7

If a width difference has been created between
the two flaps, you can re-cut the extra fabric
from one side. Move the pins if they bother you,
but do not remove them.

Make the pouch

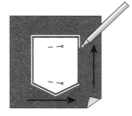 

8

Copy the pattern for the pouch, page 232, onto the
paper and pin it on the fabric.
Draw the pouch with the white pencil and cut it out.

9

With the orange thread, along the upper edge of the pouch, make a stitch
with the sewing machine ⅜ in. (1 cm) from the edge, adjusting it to the
largest point. Anchor the seam well at the beginning and end.

If the stitch is not very visible, make a second
stitch on top of the first one. Make another
stitch between the first line and the edge of the
pouch. Double it like the first one if necessary.

10

Place two pins on the front side of the pouch, ⅝ in.
(1.5 cm) from the sides, to mark out the width of the
word "YES!". Using the pattern to help you, draw the
letters directly onto the fabric with the white pencil,
starting with the E in the middle. Remove the pins.

Embroider the word

Embroider each letter using the reverse stitch by making ⁵⁄₁₆ in. (5 mm) stitches, using a 12 in. (30 cm) length of embroidery thread.

For the "Y":
Make a knot and insert the needle through the back, ⁵⁄₁₆ in. (5 mm) below the top of the left bar. Pull the thread and insert the needle at the top of the bar. Continue to the intersection. Pass through the back and take the needle out ⁵⁄₁₆ in. (5 mm) below the top of the right bar. Pull the thread and insert the needle at the top of the bar. Continue to the bottom of the bar. Make a knot on the back.

For the "E":
Start at the right end of the top bar, shifting the needle by ⁵⁄₁₆ in. (5 mm). Continue with the vertical bar, then the bottom bar. At the end of the bottom bar, go to the back and bring the needle back up, shifting it ⁵⁄₁₆ in. (5 mm) to the left of the middle bar.

For the "S" and the exclamation point:
Embroider them like the other letters, beginning at the top. Make the dot by embroidering several dots side by side.

Embroider the star

12

With the white pencil, draw a small "x" 1 in. (2.5 cm) from the tip of the pouch to identify the center of the star.

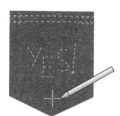

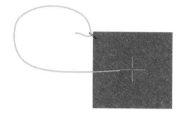

Prepare a new 12 in. (30 cm) length of thread and make a knot. Insert the needle through the back, 3/16 in. (5 mm) to the left of the white "x." Pull the thread, then insert the needle at the center of the "x."

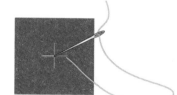

Next, pull the needle through to the right of the "x", then insert it back through in the middle. You have made two stitches face to face.

Make two more vertical stitches, then four inclined stitches between the first ones, still face to face, each time inserting the needle in the middle. Anchor the thread on the back.

Sew the pouch

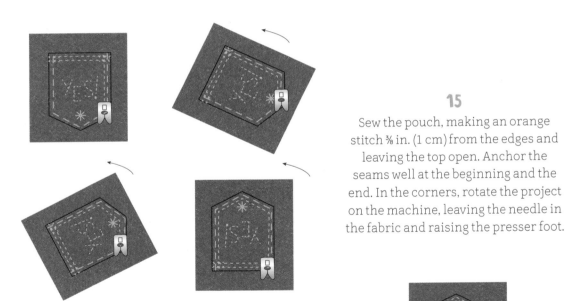

13

With the cover still on the planner, position the pouch in the middle of the front, slightly closer to the bottom. Pin the pouch.

14

Remove the planner from the cover. Remove the pins from the front flap.
Unfold the flap. Baste the pouch.

15

Sew the pouch, making an orange stitch ⅜ in. (1 cm) from the edges and leaving the top open. Anchor the seams well at the beginning and the end. In the corners, rotate the project on the machine, leaving the needle in the fabric and raising the presser foot.

16

Remove the basting from the pouch. Make a second stitch between the first one and the edge of the pouch.

Sew the flaps

17

Put the planner back in the cover and pin the flap again. Baste the flaps at the top and bottom as close as possible to the planner. Remove the pins.

18

Remove the planner and open the cover. On the front face, make a stitch at the top and bottom along the entire cover, just above the basting. Anchor the seams well at the beginning and end.

19

Make a second stitch between the first one and the edge. Remove the basting threads.

Make the bookmark

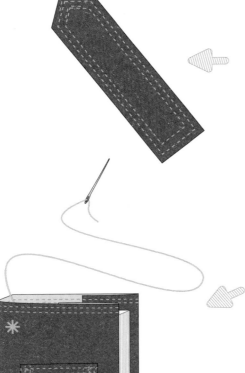

20

Like the pouch, cut the bookmark out using the pattern, following the grain carefully. Starting with the tip, stitch all the way around the bookmark, ⅜ in. (1 cm) from the edge. Next, stitch a second time, between the first stitching and the edge of the bookmark, just as you did for the pouch. Anchor the seams well at the beginning and end.

21

Prepare an 31 ½ in. (80 cm) length of embroidery thread. Make a knot at the end. In the top left, on the front of the cover, embroider a star, like the one at the bottom of the pouch. Do not cut the thread after the last stitch.

22

Insert the needle ¾ in. (2 cm) from the tip of the bookmark, from behind. Leave about 3 ⅛ in. (8 cm) of thread between the slip case and the bookmark.

23

Embroider three dots around the tip
of the bookmark. Finish with a knot
on the back. Do not cut the thread.

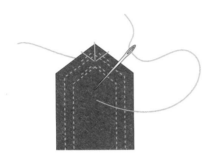

24

With the same thread, embroider a row of
reverse stitches in the middle of the bookmark.
Embroider a final star. Put the cover in place
and slide the bookmark between the pages!

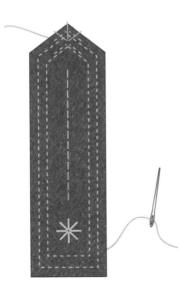

Trick

IF THE PLANNER IS
SMALLER, USE A PHOTOCOPIER TO
REDUCE THE SIZE OF THE POUCH MODEL.
YOU CAN ALSO SEW ON A REAL POCKET
FROM AN OLD PAIR OF BLUE JEANS.

Pillow cover

The back of this cover is open like a pillowcase, so you can wash it easily. The front combines quick and easy patchwork done on the sewing machine and appliqués that give it character.

You will need:

- 3 assorted light blue fabrics: 59 x 16 in. (150 x 40 cm)
  red and dark blue: 17 ¾ x 12 in. (45 x 30 cm)
- a pillow to cover measuring 16 in. (40 cm) per side

Other materials:

a pencil, a ruler, a tape measure, sewing thread (white and blue), a sewing machine, shears, pins, measure square

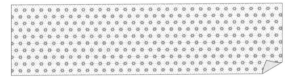

★ **Dimensions**
16 x 16 in. (40 x 40 cm)

SEE THE INTRODUCTION

COPYING A PATTERN, PAGES 18 AND 20 / DRAWING ON FABRIC, PAGE 20/PINNING, PAGE 36/ STRAIGHT STITCH, PAGE 30/BACKSTITCHING, PAGE 31/ZIGZAG STITCH, PAGE 30/ MAKING A HEM, PAGE 40/ BASTING, PAGE 37/CUTTING GUIDE, PAGE 16/ FLATTENING SEAMS, PAGE 38/NOTCHING, PAGE 39

Prepare the patterns for the triangles

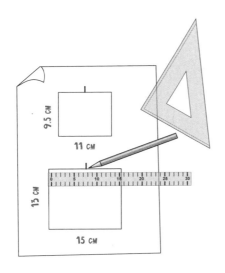

1

On the paper, draw two rectangles with the dimensions indicated in the drawing, with the ruler and square. On each rectangle, draw a reference mark in the middle of the top side.

2

Next, draw two lines that start from each reference mark going down to the bottom corners. You will end up with two triangles. Cut them out.

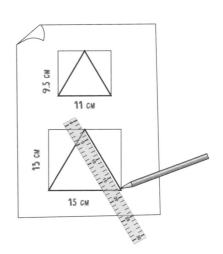

Cut out the fabrics

3

Using the cutting diagrams to help you, use a pencil to draw the various pieces you will need on the three pieces of fabric. Use your ruler and square for the squares and rectangles (see page 20) and pin the patterns for the triangles. If the fabrics you have chosen have geometric patterns like those in the pictures, follow the lines carefully to draw your pieces.

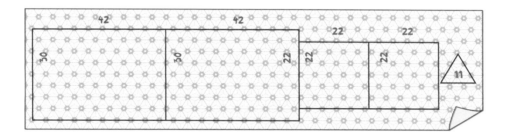

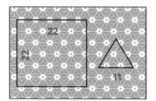

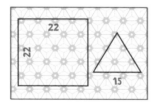

Cut out all of the pieces of fabric.

Assemble the front

4

Place a light blue square on a dark blue square, front to front, placing the pins perpendicular to the side to be assembled.

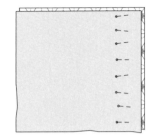

5

With the thread in a color coordinated with the fabrics, make a seam on the pinned side, ⅜ in. (1 cm) from the edge, from one edge to the other. Assemble the red square on the other light blue square in the same way.

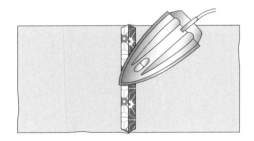

6

Remove the pins. Unfold the two strips formed and flatten the seams with your fingernail, then iron it, being careful not to burn yourself.

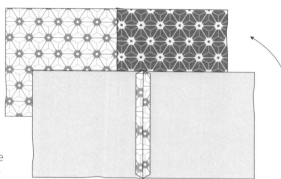

7

Paying attention to their direction so that the colors of the squares are placed correctly, place the two strips front to front. Pin perpendicular to the side to be assembled. Make sure the seams that have already been made are aligned. Make a seam ⅜ in. (1 cm) from the edge.

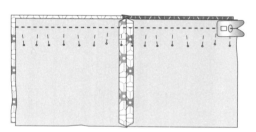

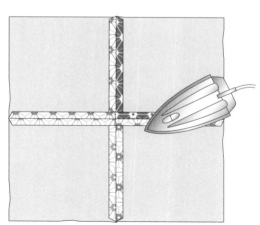

8

Remove the pins. Unfold the square and flatten the seams with your fingernail, then iron it. Your four squares are assembled!

Make a decorative seam

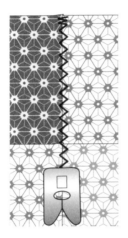

9

On the front side, with the blue thread, make a vertical seam straddling the squares, using the zigzag stitch adjusted to the widest width and a medium length. Align the center of the presser foot carefully on the border between the fabrics, and begin and end with several tighter stitches (lengthwise).

10

Make a horizontal seam straddling the squares in the same way. Keep the settings of the machine for the next step.

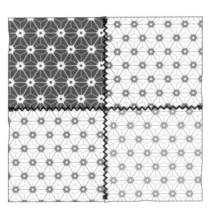

Sew the appliqués

11

Pin the large red triangle to the center of the dark blue square. Next, pin the small, light blue and dark blue triangles, superimposing them to check your layout.

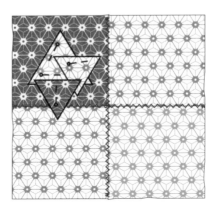

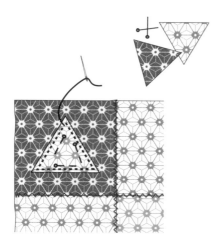

12

Remove the two small triangles and baste the large red triangle ⅜ in. (1 cm) from its edge. Remove the pins.

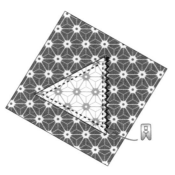

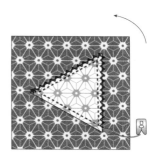

13

Sew the large triangle using the zigzag stitch with white thread and the same settings you used for the decorative seams. Begin and end with tighter stitches. In the corners, raise the presser foot while leaving the needle in the fabric, rotate the fabric, then lower the presser foot. Remove the basting thread.

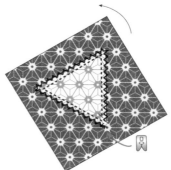

14

Sew the light blue triangle in the same way
with blue thread, then the dark blue triangle
with white thread.

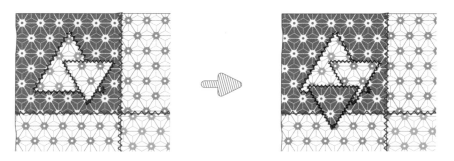

~ Prepare the back ~

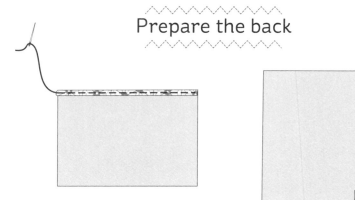

15

On the back of each large light blue rectangle,
prepare a hem on one long side by folding down
⅜ in. (1 cm), then ⅜ in. (1 cm) again.
Baste, then stitch with the machine, without
backstitching. Iron the fabric rectangles, being
careful not to burn yourself.

16

Pin one of these rectangles to the front of the cover, front to front, aligning it against the top edge. Place the hem against the center of the pillow. Stick pins on the hem as well, so that it does not move during sewing.

17

Pin the second rectangle on top, aligning it against the bottom edge and placing the hem toward the center of the pillow. The opening that makes it possible to put the pillow inside will be located between the two hems.

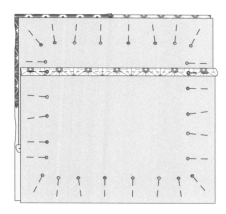

Sew the back

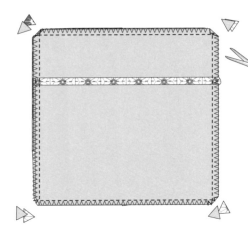

18

Make a straight seam all the way around, ⅜ in. (1 cm) from the edge. Notch the corners ⅛ in. (3 mm) from the seam. Overcast all the way around, as explained for the drawstring bag, page 127. Start the zigzag at the center of one of the sides and superimpose the last stitches on the first ones. Remove the visible pins.

Add the finishing touches

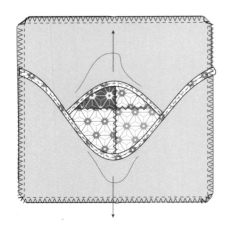

19

Push the hems back and turn the cover right-side out through the opening. Push the corners all the way out with a pencil. Remove the last pins.

20

Carefully iron the cover
front and back. Put the pillow inside.

 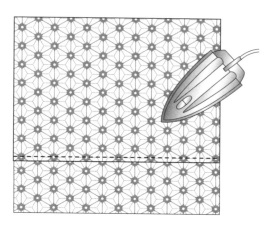

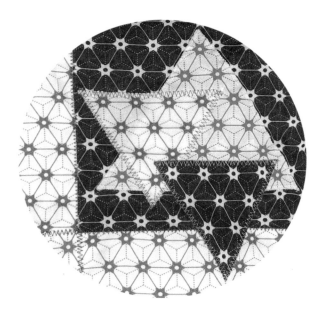

Small bins with square base

Practical for storing all of your little accessories, these lined trays are reversible. Remember this when you choose your fabrics. The inside and the outside are made using the same method and are assembled at the end.

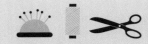

You will need:

• 2 fairly thick matching fabrics per model
For the small model:
one rectangle measuring 16 ½ x 6 ¼ in. (42 x 16 cm) and one square measuring 4 ¾ x 4 ¾ in. (12 x 12 cm) in each fabric
For the large model:
one rectangle measuring 21 ¼ x 8 in. (54 x 20 cm) and one square measuring 6 x 6 in. (15 x 15 cm) in each fabric

Advice: Be sure to cut your pieces as precisely as possible, referring to the explanations on page 20. If you use fabrics with large or geometric patterns, take this into account when you draw the pieces.

Other materials:

matching sewing thread, a sewing machine, a needle, shears, a ruler, a pencil, an embroidery needle

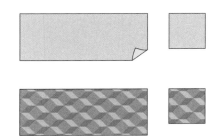

★ Dimensions of the folded lining
Small model: 4 x 4 in. (10 x 10 cm)
Large model: 5 ¼ x 5 ¼ in. (13 x 13 cm)

 SEE THE INTRODUCTION

BASTING, PAGE 37 / OVERCAST STITCH, PAGE 25 / HEMSTITCH, PAGE 25 / STRAIGHT STITCH, PAGE 30 / ZIGZAG STITCH, PAGE 30 / FRONT TO FRONT, PAGE 36 / BACKSTITCH, PAGE 31 / FLATTEN THE SEAMS, PAGE 38

Draw the seam lines

1

On the back of the first large rectangle, draw a line ⅜ in. (1 cm) from the short sides.

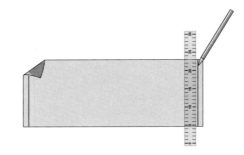

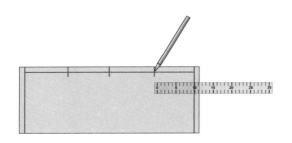

2

Draw a line ⅜ in. (1 cm) from one long side between the two lines on the short sides. On this line, make three 4 in. (10 cm) reference marks for the small model, or 5 ¼ in. (13 cm) for the large model. These are the reference marks for the corners of the bin.

Advice

THE LINE DRAWN ON THE LONG SIDE OF THE RECTANGLE REPRESENTS THE BOTTOM OF THE PERIMETER OF THE BIN. TAKE THIS INTO ACCOUNT DEPENDING ON THE PATTERN OF THE FABRIC YOU HAVE CHOSEN.

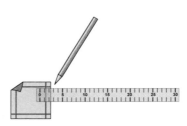

3

On the back of the square of the same fabric, draw a line ⅜ in. (1 cm) from the four sides.

Form the perimeter of the bin

4

Fold the rectangle in half widthwise, front to front. Pin the short side, then baste ⅛ in. to ³⁄₁₆ in. (3 mm to 5 mm) from the pencil line.

5

Sew on the pencil line, anchoring the stitch well at the beginning and end. You will end up with a tube. Remove the basting thread.

6

Flatten the seams with your fingernail or an iron.

Baste the bottom

7

Pull the tube through so it is right-side out and once again draw the three reference marks for the corners, but on the front face.

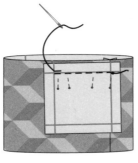

8

Place the seam of the tube in front of you. Pin the square on top, front to front, aligning the edges well, and aligning the right line on the seam and the left line on the reference mark.

9

With a thread the same color as the fabric, baste this side of the square between the two reference marks only, sewing on the pencil line. Make an additional stitch in the corner so that it does not move.

10

Remove the pins. Rotate the square to bring the next corner onto the following reference mark of the tube and pin it.

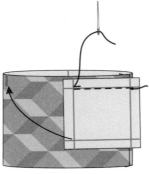

11

Baste like the first side and don't forget the extra stitch in the corner.

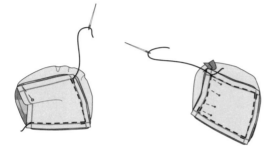

12

Baste the other two sides of the square. Always begin by pinning the corner, since this becomes more difficult. The tube moves toward the back.

Sew the bottom with the machine

13

Placing the tube on the top, stitch with the machine on the basting, with a thread of the same color. Start in the middle of one side with a few backstitches. Rotate in the corners, leaving the needle in the fabric and raising the presser foot. Finish going around the perimeter with a few backstitches.

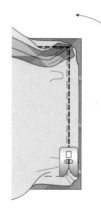

14

Remove the basting thread if it is not too caught up in the seam and if it can be seen on the front; otherwise, leave it.

Make the other face of the bin

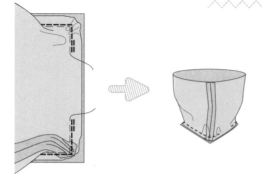

15

With the other fabric, repeat steps 1 to 14, but leave a 2 in. (5 cm) opening in the middle of one of the sides of the square. If you have chosen to leave the basting, remove it from the opening.

Assemble the two faces of the bin

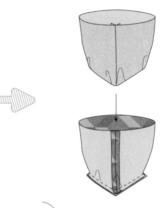

16

Turn over one of the two assemblies so that it is right-side up. Put the one that is right-side up inside the one that is inside-out (they are then front to front), aligning the two side seams.

17

Pin and baste ³⁄₁₆ in. (5 mm) from the edge.

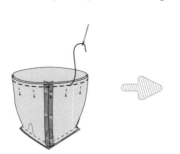

18

Stitch ⅜ in. (1 cm) from the edge, starting and ending the seam with backstitches.

19

Remove the inside assembly.

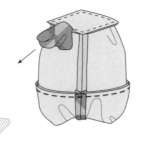

20

Through the opening left on one of the squares, reverse the assembly so it is right-side out.

21

Close the opening by hand, using an overcast stitch.

22

Put one face in the other. Choose whichever one you want: the bin is reversible!

24

Baste the edge at ⅝ in. (1.5 cm) from the top.

23

Flatten the edge with your fingernail, then with an iron.

25

Make a top stitch using a zigzag stitch between the basting and the edge, starting at the seam and ending with backstitching overlapping the beginning.

26

Remove the basting. Fold down the brim to form the lining.

Fox pillow

This pillow is as soft as a stuffed animal.
Made from fake fur, it's easy to sew.

You will need:

- 31 ½ x 16 in. (80 x 40 cm) of orange fake fur
- 19 ½ x 16 in. (50 x 40 cm) of white fake fur
- one bag of synthetic filling
- 2 buttons with a diameter of 1 ⅛ in. (3 cm)
- 1 button with a diameter of ⅝ in. (1.5 cm)

Other materials:

one sheet of tracing paper, a grease pencil or dark marker, pins (with colored heads so you can see them well against the fur), orange sewing thread, a sewing machine, a needle, shears, a ruler, a square, a pencil

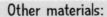

★ Dimensions
13 in. (33 cm) per side, not including the ears and tail

SEE THE INTRODUCTION

COPYING A PATTERN, PAGES 18 AND 20 / PINNING, PAGE 36 / HEMSTITCH, PAGE 25 / OVERCAST STITCH, PAGE 25 / FRONT TO FRONT, PAGE 36 / CUTTING GUIDE, PAGE 16

Cut out the pieces of fabric

1

With the pencil, copy the patterns for the ears and tail, page 233, onto the tracing paper.

2

Cut them out.

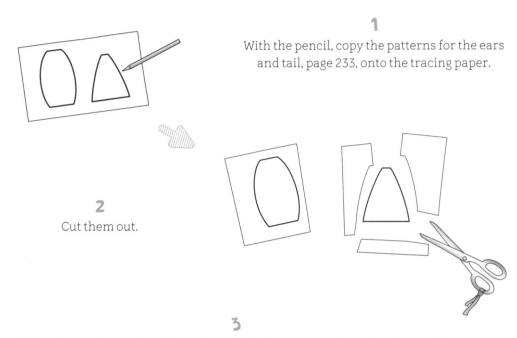

3

Using the cutting guides below, identify the best way to place the pieces to be cut on the two pieces of fur. Start by placing the large pieces (here, the two squares and the triangle). So that you are able to draw correctly, you should place the pattern pieces with the back of the fur facing you.

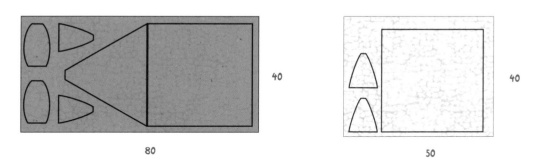

40

80

40

50

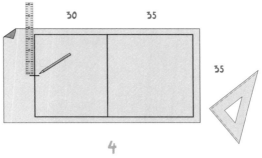

4

On the back of the orange fur, first use the grease pencil or marker to draw a 13 ¾ x 13 ¾ in. (35 x 35 cm) square, then a 12 x 13 ¾ in. (30 x 35 cm) rectangle, alongside this square. Make a reference mark in the middle of the left side of the rectangle. Draw the diagonals starting from this reference mark. Cut the tip using a line located 1 ⅛ in. (3 cm) from the tip.

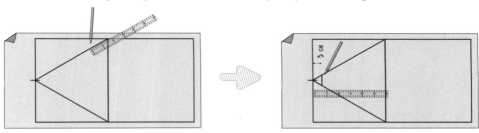

5

Next, copy the pattern for the tail twice and the pattern for the ears twice, still on the back of the orange fur. On the back of the white fur, draw a 13 ¾ x 13 ¾ in. (35 x 35 cm) square and the pattern for the ears twice. Cut out the pieces.

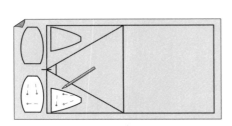

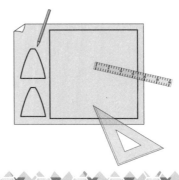

Prepare the face of the pillow

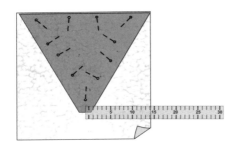

6

Place the orange triangle on the white square, aligning it against the edge, and fasten it using pins about 1 ⅛ in. (3 cm) from the edges. Since fabric is flexible, check that the tip of the triangle is centered correctly by measuring with the ruler.

7

Fold the two diagonals of the triangle ⅜ in. (1 cm) toward the back and move the pins toward the edge to hold the hem you just made. Next, fold the tip of the triangle in the same way and pin it.

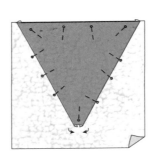

Advice

CHOOSE COLORFUL PINS THAT WILL STAND OUT ON THE FUR BECAUSE THEY WILL SINK INTO IT.

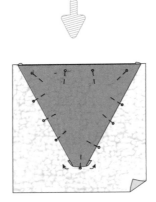

8

Sew the diagonals and the tip of the triangle by hand using a hemstitch, from one corner of the square to the other.

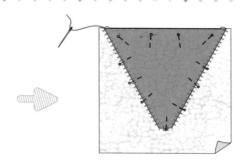

Prepare the ears and tail

9

Pin the two pieces of one ear (one white and one orange) front to front. Baste them ⅝ in. (1.5 cm) from the edge and sew them with the machine ⅜ in. (1 cm) from the edge, except on the bottom. Begin and end with backstitches. Sew the other ear and the tail in the same way. Remove the basting.

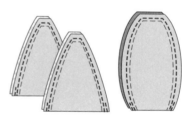

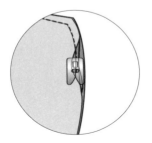 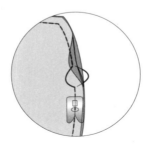

Advice

⚡ THE FAKE FUR IS SUPPLE AND MAY WIND AROUND THE PRESSER FOOT. IN THIS CASE, RAISE THE PRESSER FOOT, MOVE THE FABRIC AWAY WITH THE TIP OF THE SHEARS, PULL THE THREAD AND RESUME SEWING A BIT FARTHER DOWN, KNOWING THAT YOU MAY NEED TO TOUCH UP YOUR WORK BY HAND LATER.

177

10

Reverse the ears and the tail to turn them right-side out, and fill them with synthetic filling, pushing it in with a pencil.

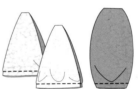

11

Close the opening: baste ⅝ in. (1.5 cm) from the edge, then stitch at ⅜ in. (1 cm), with no backstitching. Remove the basting.

Assemble the two faces of the pillow

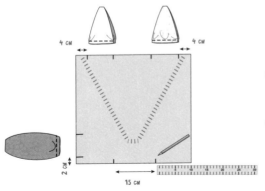

12

On the back of the face of the pillow, make reference marks with the marker close to the edges for the openings: two marks 6 in. (15 cm) apart at the bottom to reverse the pillow; two marks for the width of the tail on the left side, ¾ in. (2 cm) from the bottom; two marks for the width of the ears at the top, at 1 ½ in. (4 cm) on each side.

13

Pin the face of the pillow on the orange square, front to front. Check that you can fit the ears and the tail into the openings. Baste the four corners of the pillow at ⅝ in. (1.5 cm) from the edge, then sew them at ⅜ in. (1 cm), leaving the four openings (between the marks). Stop and start the seam at each mark with backstitches. At the top of the square, you must sew through three layers (the two squares and the triangle). If necessary, help the machine advance by turning the hand wheel.

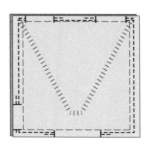

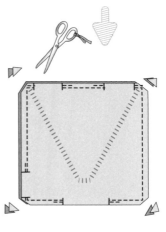

14

Remove the basting. Notch the corners, making sure not to cut too close to the seam.

15

Reverse the pillow through the 6 in. (15 cm) opening, to turn it right-side out. Push the corners out with the ruler.

Sew the ears and tail, then the eyes

16

Put the ears and tail ⅜ in. (1 cm) into the provided openings, so as to hide the seam. Pin them. Sew them by hand on the front and back of the pillow using an overcast stitch.

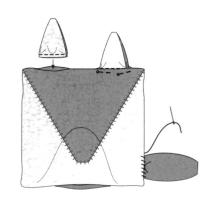

17

Once the tail has been sewn, straighten it and hold it to the side of the pillow with a few extra stitches.

18

Fill the pillow with synthetic filling.

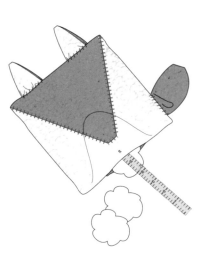

19

Close the opening by hand, using an overcast stitch.

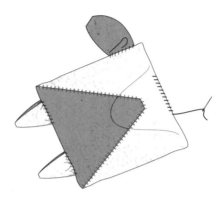

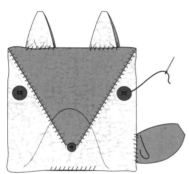

20

Sew the large buttons for the eyes and the small button for the muzzle.

Funny charms

With fabric scraps, make these charms and invent new ones.
Ideally, choose fabrics with small patterns.

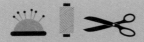

You will need:

- for each charm: 2 rectangles of fabric measuring about 4 x 6 in. (10 x 15 cm)
- string:
  yellow charm: 4 of 6 in. (15 cm) for the limbs and 1 of 2 in. (5 cm) for the nose
  blue charm: 4 of 6 in. (15 cm) for the limbs and 5 of 1 ½ in. (4 cm) for the hair
  orange charm: 5 of 1 ¾ in. (4.5 cm) (4 for the limbs and 1 for the hair)
  flower charm: 4 of 2 in. (5 cm) for the limbs and 2 of 6 in. (15 cm) for the antennas
  charm with skulls: 5 of 1 ¾ in. (4.5 cm) (4 for the limbs and 1 for the smile)
- buttons
- a little bit of synthetic filling

Other materials:

paper, a pencil, matching thread, a sewing machine (optional), a needle, shears, pins, fabric glue

★ Dimensions
About 3 ⅛ in. (8 cm) x 6 in. (15 cm)

SEE THE INTRODUCTION

COPYING A PATTERN, PAGES 18 AND 20 / PINNING, PAGE 36 / BASTING, PAGE 37 / STRAIGHT STITCH, PAGE 30 / REVERSE STITCH, PAGE 24 / NOTCHING, PAGE 39 / OVERCAST STITCH, PAGE 25 / SEWING BUTTONS, PAGE 46 / CROSS-STITCH, PAGE 49 / FRONT TO FRONT, PAGE 36

Prepare the face of the charm

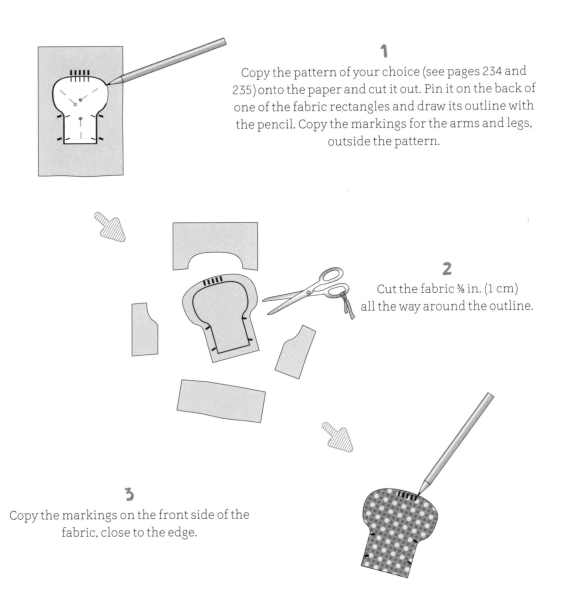

1

Copy the pattern of your choice (see pages 234 and 235) onto the paper and cut it out. Pin it on the back of one of the fabric rectangles and draw its outline with the pencil. Copy the markings for the arms and legs, outside the pattern.

2

Cut the fabric ⅜ in. (1 cm) all the way around the outline.

3

Copy the markings on the front side of the fabric, close to the edge.

Attach the string

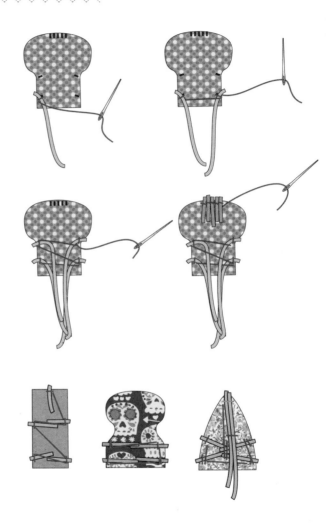

4

Leaving a tail of ⅜ in. (1 cm) on the outside, attach the strings on the front side of the fabric at the pencil markings using a few quick stitches by hand. These attachments are temporary: use a contrasting thread that will be easy for you to see and sew all of the strings in a row without cutting the thread.

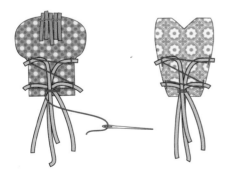

5

Gather the strings at the center of the fabric. To avoid catching them in the assembly seam, attach them using a stitch. If needed, wind them or have them hang down below the bottom, since they will not be sewn. Anchor and cut the thread.

Sew the two faces.

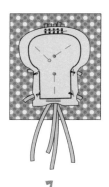

6

Pin the prepared face on the other fabric rectangle, front to front.

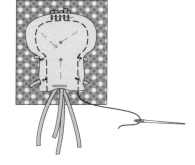

7

Sew, following the pencil outline, except on the bottom. Use a straight stitch (on the machine) or a reverse stitch (by hand). If you are sewing on the machine, baste beforehand. By hand, make sure to catch the strings securely in the stitches.

8

Cut out the second face by following the outline of the first.

9

Remove the pins and the threads fastening the strings that are visible on this side. Depending on the model you have chosen, notch the rounded parts and the corners, except those on the bottom.

Advice

ON STRAIGHT LINES, SEWING
WITH THE MACHINE IS FASTER AND MORE
SOLID. ON SMALL, DETAILED PIECES,
HOWEVER, SEWING BY HAND
IS OFTEN EASIER.

Finish the body

10

Pull the charm through the opening at the bottom so it is right-side out. If needed, pull gently on the strings.

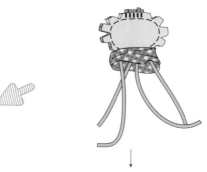

11

Remove the temporary threads if any are left. Gently push on the corners and rounded areas with a pencil.

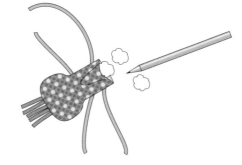

12

Fill the charm with filling, in small packets. Push them with the pencil.

13

Fold the bottom of the body inward just below the two strings and sew it using the overcast stitch.

187

Finish the charms

14

Cut the strings cleanly. Drawing inspiration from the models, finish them in different ways: you can dip the ends in a bit of glue so they do not fray. On long strings, make a knot first. Conversely, you can fray some of the strings.

15

Sew buttons for the eyes.

16

For the yellow charm, make the mouth by sewing a string folded in half, using several stitches on top of one another.

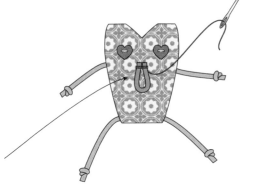

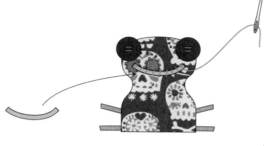

17

For the charm with the skulls, make the mouth by sewing an overcast stitch straddling a string forming a semicircle.

18

For the charm with flowers, make the eyes by sewing two buttons on top of each other: sew the first button on the charm, then the second button on the whole thing.

For the mouth, make a cross-stitch. Make a knot at the end of a 12 in. (30 cm) length of thread and insert it through the back of the charm. Have it come out the front and make a cross-stitch. Finish with several small stitches on top of one another on the back and put a dot of glue.

Lined tote bag

This bag, made up of two pockets set one within the other, is beautiful both inside and outside, and is reversible. The inside is darker, since it is completely spotted. But you are free to combine the fabrics any way you like!

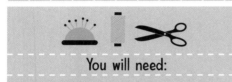

You will need:

- 16 x 31 ½ in. (40 x 80 cm) of patterned fabric
- 31 ½ x 35 ½ in. (80 x 90 cm) of spotted fabric
- for the charm: fabric scraps, embroidery thread and about 12 in. (30 cm) of thin ribbon.

Other materials:

a pencil, a 16 in. (40 cm) ruler, matching thread, a sewing machine, a needle, shears, pins, a safety pin

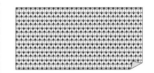

★ **Dimensions not including the handles**
Width 12 in. (30 cm) x height 14 in. (36 cm)
Length of the handles: 13 ¼ in. (34 cm)

SEE THE INTRODUCTION

DRAWING ON FABRIC, PAGE 16 / PINNING, PAGE 36 / FRONT TO FRONT, PAGE 36 / STRAIGHT STITCH, PAGE 30 / BACKSTITCH, PAGE 31 / OVERCAST STITCH, PAGE 25 / FLATTENING SEAMS, PAGE 38 / NOTCHING, PAGE 39

Cut the fabric

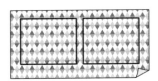

1

Draw all of the pieces on the fabrics based on the dimensions given below and following the cutting guides here so you do not risk running out of fabric. For geometric patterns (like diamonds) or repeating patterns (like polka dots), align the drawing based on the patterns, rather than the edge of the fabric.

Advice

THE WIDTH OF ALL OF THE RECTANGLES THAT MAKE UP THE POCKETS IS 12 ½ IN. (32 CM). MAKE SURE TO CUT THEM IN THE RIGHT DIRECTION TO PLACE THE PATTERNS AS PLANNED. DEPENDING ON THE FABRICS YOU HAVE CHOSEN AND THE DIRECTION YOU WOULD LIKE FOR THE PATTERNS, YOU MAY NEED TO CHANGE THE CUTTING GUIDE. IF SO, MAKE A DRAWING FIRST TO AVOID MISTAKES.

Outer pocket:
Draw and cut out two patterned rectangles of 12 ½ x 10 ½ in. (32 x 27 cm) and two spotted rectangles of 12 ½ x 5 in. (32 x 13 cm).

Inner pocket:
Draw and cut out two large spotted rectangles of 12 ½ x 15 in. (32 x 38 cm).

Handles:
Draw and cut out two long spotted strips of 3 ⅛ x 29 ½ in. (8 cm x 75 cm).

Prepare the faces of the outer pocket

2

Pin the long side of a small spotted rectangle to the long side of a rectangle with diamonds, front to front, placing the pins perpendicularly, ¾ in. (2 cm) from the edge.

3

Make a seam along the edge, at ⅜ in. (1 cm). This seam will be simple and straight; it is not necessary to baste.

4

Unfold the rectangles and flatten the seams with your fingernail or with an iron. Make the second face the same way.

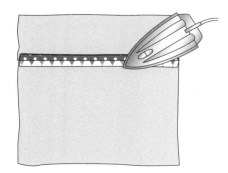

Assemble the outer pocket

5

Pin the flaps of the seams to hold them securely. Place both faces of the outer pocket against each other, front to front, aligning the seams.

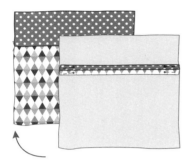  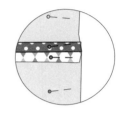

Place pins perpendicularly on the two long sides
and the bottom small side.

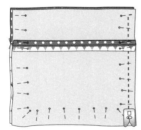  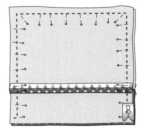

6

Sew the three pinned sides, ⅜ in. (1 cm) from the edge.
In the corners, proceed as explained on page 35.

Assemble the inner pocket

7

Sew, front to front, the two large spotted rectangles, on three sides, as for the outer pocket.

Make the handles

8

Fold a large spotted strip in half lengthwise, front to front, aligning the edges carefully. Pin the long side. Sew it ⅜ in. (1 cm) from the edge. You will end up with a tube.

9

Reverse the tube so it is right-side out as explained on pages 44 and 45.

10

Flatten the handle with the iron. The seam must stay well-aligned with one side.

11

Make an overcast stitch along the two long sides, 3⁄16 in. (5 mm) from the edges. This extra stitch gives a bit more strength to the handles, but it is optional. Make the second handle in the same way.

Assemble the bag

12

Reverse the outer pocket to turn it right-side out and iron it.

13

Fold the handles in half, making sure not to twist them. Pin the two ends of the handles on each face, 2 ⅜ in. (6 cm) from the sides of the pocket, leaving a tail of ⅜ in. (1 cm).

Place the pins perpendicular to the edge of the pocket, ¾ in. (2 cm) from the edge.

Also pin the folds of the handles on the pockets so that the handles do not move during sewing.

14

Place the outer pocket
in the inner pocket.

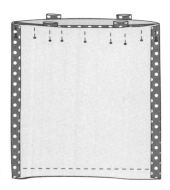

15

Pin the edge of the two pockets together,
flattening the flaps of the seams. The
handles are between the two pockets.

16

Make a seam ⅜ in. (1 cm) from the
edge, leaving an opening on one face
between the two ends of a handle.
Anchor the seams well at the
beginning and end.

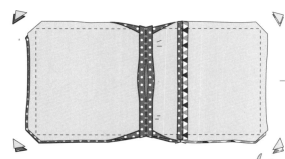

17

Take out the outer pocket. Both
pockets will be inside out. Notch the
corners ³⁄₁₆ in. (5 mm) from the seam.

Finishing touches

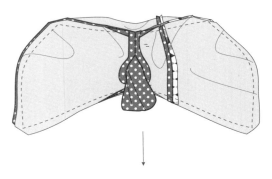

18

Reverse the whole thing through the opening on one of the faces, at the handle.

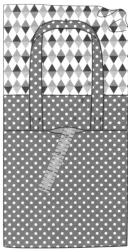

19

Both pockets should be right-side out. Push the corners of the outer pocket with a long object, such as a pencil or a ruler. Iron the pockets.

20

Place the inner pocket in the outer pocket. Push the corners with a long object.

Fold down the edges of the opening toward the inside, so as to align it with the top of the bag that has already been sewn. Close the opening by hand using an overcast stitch. Use a thread the same color as the fabric and make the stitches as discreet as possible.

22

Remove the pins that are holding the handles. Raise the handles upward and flatten the edge of the bag with your fingernail or an iron. Make an overcast stitch along the edge, at ³⁄₁₆ in. (5 mm). Superimpose the beginning and end points over ¾ in. (2 cm) to anchor the seam securely, at the seam on one side.

Charm

You can decorate your bag with a ribbon and can sew on matching flower blossoms (see pages 64 through 69).

Tutu-style skirt

Learn to make gathers for this skirt made to your measurements.
A tulle tutu is worn over a slightly shorter opaque cotton slip.
An elastic belt makes it possible to adjust the fit.

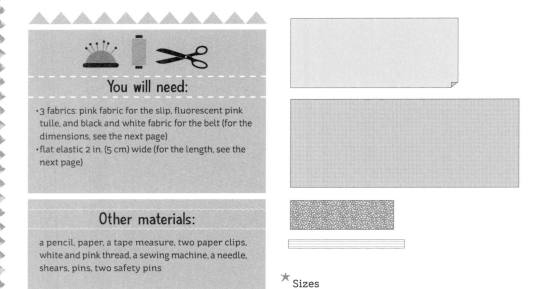

You will need:

- 3 fabrics: pink fabric for the slip, fluorescent pink tulle, and black and white fabric for the belt (for the dimensions, see the next page)
- flat elastic 2 in. (5 cm) wide (for the length, see the next page)

Other materials:

a pencil, paper, a tape measure, two paper clips, white and pink thread, a sewing machine, a needle, shears, pins, two safety pins

★ **Sizes**
8 to 14 years

SEE THE INTRODUCTION

MAKING GATHERS, PAGE 41 / BASTING, PAGE 37 / STRAIGHT STITCH, PAGE 30 / BACKSTITCH, PAGE 31 / PINNING, PAGE 36 / FRONT TO FRONT, PAGE 36 / FLATTENING SEAMS, PAGE 38 / MAKING A HEM, PAGE 40 / OVERCAST STITCH, PAGE 25

Take your measurements

1

With the tape measure, measure your waist size loosely, i.e., the narrowest place where you usually wear your belt. Measure your hips, i.e., the widest location at the buttocks so you can put the skirt on without forcing it. Also measure the length from your waist to your knee (or the length you want for the pink slip).

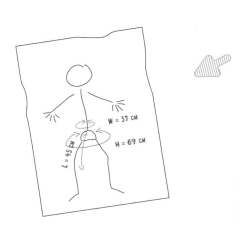

Write the measurements down on a piece of paper (you can have fun making a sketch):
W = your waist
H = your hips
L = the length from the waist

For information, here is a size chart (in centimeters) that may help you. However, if you take your measurements carefully, your skirt will be made perfectly to your specifications.

Average size/age	8	10	12	14
W (waist)	56	59	62	64
H (hips)	68	74	83	88
L (waist-knee length)	44	49	54	59

2

Calculate the fabric dimensions that you need and write them down on a piece of paper.
Solid pink cotton (slip): 43 ¼ in. (110 cm) x L
Fluorescent pink tulle (tutu): 59 in. (150 cm) x (L + 4 ¾ in. (12 cm)
Black and white fabric (belt): (H + 4 in. (10 cm)) x 8 in. (20 cm)
Elastic: W + 8 in. (20 cm)

Cut the fabrics to the right dimensions.

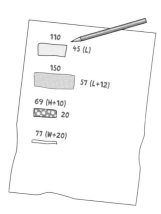

Prepare the slip

3

Adjust the sewing machine
to the medium zigzag stitch. Overcast the small
sides of the fabric of the slip (pink fabric).

2 CM   2 CM

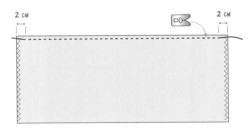

4

Set the sewing machine to the largest straight stitch. Along one of the long
sides of the fabric, make a stitch ⅜ in. (1 cm) from the edge: start and end your
seam ¾ in. (2 cm) from each side, leaving a 4 in. (10 cm) tail (on top and bottom).
You will want to pull the threads and make gathers, so do not backstitch.

5

Make a second stitch ⅜ in. (1 cm) below the first.

6

Measure half the length of the pink fabric with the tape measure, and place a pin as a reference mark.

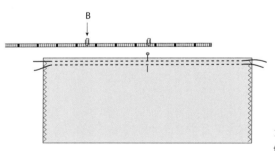

7

On the tape measure, place a paper clip to identify the length B, then another paper clip in the middle. Place the tape measure on top of the fabric, aligning the second paper clip on top of the pin. This will give you the dimensions of the fabric when it is gathered later.

Gather the slip

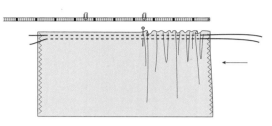

8

Holding the bottom threads on the right side, slide the fabric to gather it to the pin, gently so you do not break the threads. Distribute the gathers.

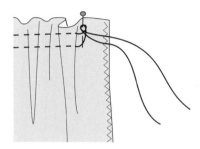

9

Insert a pin into the edge of the fabric and wind the two threads around it to block them in place.

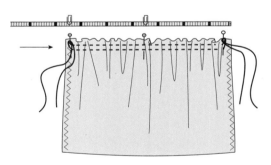

10

Gather the left side as far as the first paper clip (and block the threads in place around a pin). Place the fabric for the belt on top of the pink fabric that you have gathered: they should be the same length. Adjust the gathers if necessary.

11

Make a double knot between the gathering threads and cut them. Remove the pins.

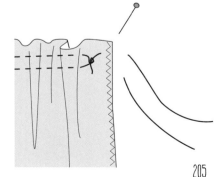

Gather and overlay the tutu

12

Gather the tulle as you did for the slip in order to obtain the same width.

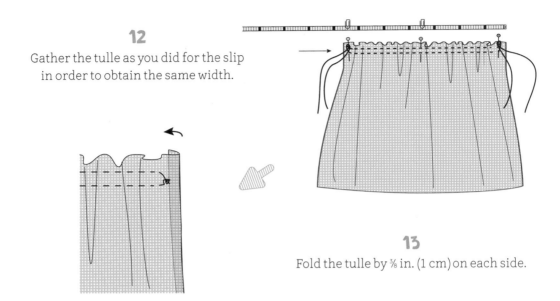

13

Fold the tulle by ⅜ in. (1 cm) on each side.

14

Pin the tulle onto the pink fabric, superimposing the gathered edges.
At each end, the pink fabric of the slip protrudes by ⅜ in. (1 cm).
Make a seam between the two gathering threads, from one end to the other.
It is not necessary to backstitch, but do not cut the threads flush with the fabric.

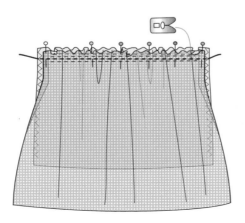

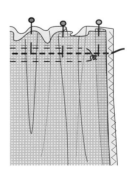

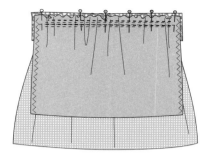

Assemble the belt

15

Superimpose the tulle + pink fabric assembly
on the strip for the belt, edge to edge:
place the tulle side against the front side
of the strip for the belt. Pin everything together.

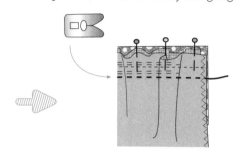

16

Make a seam ³⁄₁₆ in. (5 mm) below the gathering
threads, from one end to the other. It is not
necessary to backstitch, but do not cut the
threads flush with the fabric.

Close the skirt

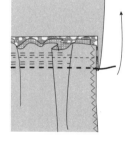

17

Unfold the belt.

18

Fold the skirt in half, front to front.
Carefully overlay the ends of the junction
between the belt and the other fabrics. Pin
the two edges, after having moved the tulle
away so it is not pinned with them. Sew the
seams ³⁄₈ in. (1 cm) away from the edge. The
seam passes just next to the folded tulle.

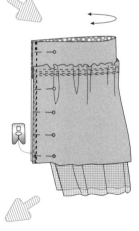

19

You will now have a tube.
Flatten the seams with your fingernail.

Make the casing for the belt

20

Fold the belt, back to back over ⅜ in. (1 cm). You can iron the fold so it is clean, but be careful not to touch the tulle with the iron.

21

Fold the belt in half on the back side of the skirt, aligning the edge on the lowest seam. The belt will hide all of the seams and the gathering threads.
Baste the belt close to the edge.

22

Turn the skirt right-side out. Slide the belt under the presser foot, at the back. Stitch the belt all the way around, several millimeters from the bottom, overlapping the first and last stitches. Make a stitch ³⁄₁₆ in. (5 mm) from the top, in the same way.

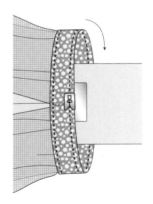

23

Turn the skirt back inside out. Unstitch the seam between the two stitches on the inner side of the skirt.

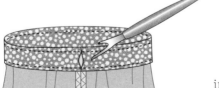

Insert the elastic

24

Insert a safety pin at each end of the flat elastic and place one end in the casing. Push it to slide the elastic into the casing.

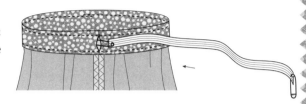

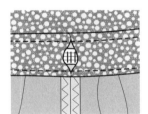

25

Use the other safety pin to keep the second end outside. Pull it until only ¾ in. (2 cm) is still protruding and fasten it temporarily (but solidly) with a few large stitches in the casing. Make sure to move the edges away from the casing so that you sew only on the inside. Remove the safety pin and place the protruding part in the casing.

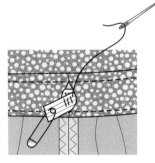

26

Remove the first safety pin through the other side of the casing. Sew the other end of the elastic in the inside of the casing, superimposing it on the first one. First, put the skirt on and pull on the elastic to adjust its length.

Advice

IF THE ELASTIC IS TOO LONG, DON'T CUT IT BEFORE YOU PUT IT IN THE CASING. IF YOU NEED TO MAKE THE SKIRT BIGGER ONE DAY, YOU CAN SIMPLY UNSTITCH THE CASING AND ADJUST THE ELASTIC.

Add the finishing touches to the belt

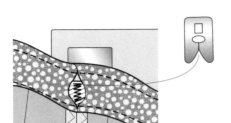

27

Put the belt back under the presser foot of the sewing machine and sew both layers of the elastic in the casing, using a tight zigzag stitch. Be careful not to catch the edges of the casing in the seam. Remove the stitches made by hand on the front side of the belt.

28

Close the casing by hand using an overcast stitch.

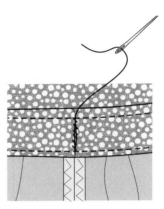

Hem the slip

29

Turn the skirt right-side out. Flip the tulle up and pin it out of your way.

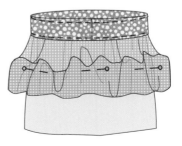

30

Turn the skirt inside-out and prepare the hem:
make a ⅝ in. (1.5 cm) fold, back to back,
then a second one.

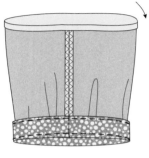

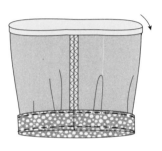

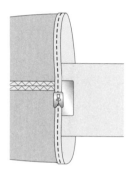

Stitch the hem with the machine, using a
straight stitch on the back.

Make a butterfly knot

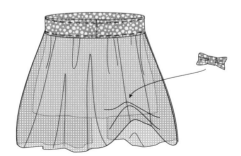

With a fabric scrap, cut a 7 ½ x 4 in. (19 x 10 cm)
rectangle and another 2 x 3 ½ in. (5 x 9 cm)
rectangle. Make a butterfly knot as explained
on pages 70 through 75. Lift a little of the tulle
tutu, make a few horizontal folds and sew the
butterfly knot onto the folds.

Lined pencil case

A good size, this case can accommodate markers, important papers, makeup, etc. While making it, you will learn to sew a zipper.

You will need:

- 2 rectangles of somewhat thick fabric measuring 9 x 13 ¾ in. (23 x 35 cm): one for the outside and one for the inner lining of the case (you can choose them in the colors shown or different colors)
- a 8 in. (20 cm) zipper
- a 9 ¾ in. (25 cm) string
- a large bead that the string can pass through

Other materials:

matching sewing thread, a sewing machine, pins, a needle, shears

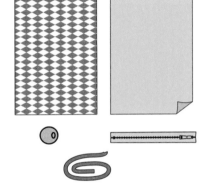

★ Dimensions
8 ¼ x 6 ¼ in. (21 x 16 cm)

SEE THE INTRODUCTION

DRAWING ON FABRIC, PAGE 20 / BASTING, PAGE 37 / FRONT TO FRONT, PAGE 36 / STRAIGHT STITCH, PAGE 30 / BACKSTITCH, PAGE 31 / FLATTENING THE SEAMS, PAGE 38 / HEMSTITCH, PAGE 25

Sew the zipper on the outer case

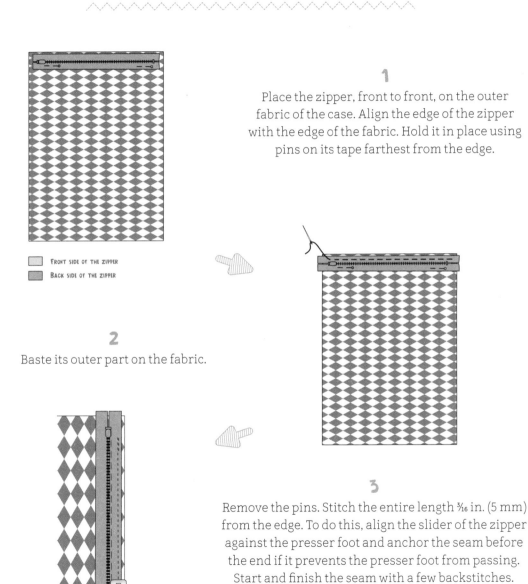

1

Place the zipper, front to front, on the outer fabric of the case. Align the edge of the zipper with the edge of the fabric. Hold it in place using pins on its tape farthest from the edge.

FRONT SIDE OF THE ZIPPER
BACK SIDE OF THE ZIPPER

2

Baste its outer part on the fabric.

3

Remove the pins. Stitch the entire length ³⁄₁₆ in. (5 mm) from the edge. To do this, align the slider of the zipper against the presser foot and anchor the seam before the end if it prevents the presser foot from passing. Start and finish the seam with a few backstitches.

4

Remove the basting and move the fabric rectangle away to free the zipper.

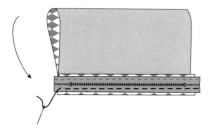

5

Fold down the edge of the fabric on the other part of the zipper, then baste after pinning. This will give you a tube.

Advice

MODERN SEWING MACHINES HAVE A SPECIAL PRESSER FOOT THAT MAKES IT POSSIBLE TO STITCH EVERYTHING AGAINST THE TEETH OF THE SLIDER. FOR THIS TYPE OF CASE, YOU CAN EASILY DO WITHOUT THIS, SINCE IT IS PREFERABLE TO OFFSET THE STITCHING.

6

Stitch with the machine, aligning the slider of the zipper against the presser foot like before. Make sure the tube is kept far enough away to sew only the slider and the edge of the fabric. Remove the basting thread.

Close the sides

7

Flatten the fabric to form a pouch. At the end of the zipper, ³⁄₁₆ in. (5 mm) after the pull tab, make two or three stitches by hand so that the ends stay connected when you open the zipper. You should be stitching on the back side, while the pull tab is hidden inside: do not mix up your sides!

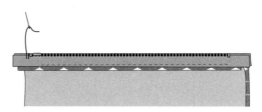

8

Slipping your fingers inside the tube, slide the pull tab to open the zipper halfway. This will allow you to reverse the case after you have sewn it.

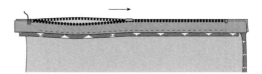

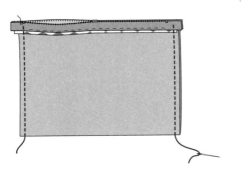

9

Baste both sides of the tube, ³⁄₁₆ in. (5 mm) from the edge, to form a pouch. For each side, start from the top of the case, to be sure that both parts of the zipper are placed correctly.

10

Sew with the machine, at ⅜ in. (1 cm) from the edge, starting from the bottom of the case. If you are unable to sew on the zipper, stop before then. Do not forget to anchor your seams securely at the beginning and end. Remove the basting threads.

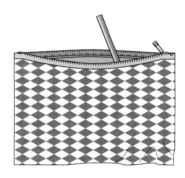

11

Open the zipper completely and reverse the case to turn it right-side out. Push the corners with a pencil. Check that the zipper closes correctly. Iron the case.

Make the lining

12

Fold the second fabric in half, front to front. Pin
and baste the sides, then sew ⅜ in.
(1 cm) from the edge. Anchor the seams well at
the beginning and end.

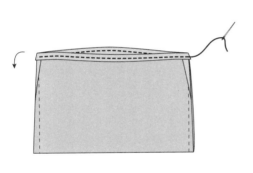

13

On the back, make a ⅜ in. (1 cm) fold and baste it.

14

Place the lining, still inside-out,
in the case.

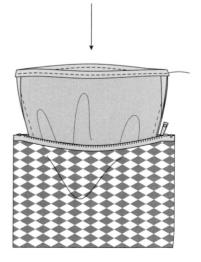

15

Sew the edge of the lining inside the case, on the zipper, ⅜ in. (1 cm) from the zipper, using a hemstitch after basting. Remove both basting threads.

16

On each face, make an overcast stitch ⅜ in. (1 cm) from the edge of the fabric to keep the lining inside. Depending on your taste, choose a thread color that will be invisible or, if you prefer, contrasting. This overcast stitch begins and ends ¾ in. (2 cm) from the sides. To make it, slide the plate of the sewing machine into the open case.

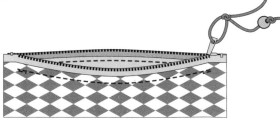

17

Place the string in the hole of the pull tab, fold it and make a knot. Slip the bead onto one strand and make a knot at the end.

Apron

With a pattern in both child and adult sizes, this apron will teach you to place piping and sew coated fabric.

You will need:

For the apron
- coated fabric: 27 ½ x 43 ¼ in. (70 x 110 cm) for the child-sized apron and 35 ½ x 43 ¼ in. (90 x 110 cm) for the adult-sized apron
- matching piping: 19 ft. 8 ¼ in. (6 m) for the child-sized apron and 21 ft. 7 ¾ in. (6.60 m) for the adult-sized apron

For the headband
- 4 in. (10 cm) of flat elastic and 35 ½ in. (90 cm) of matching piping

For the scrunchie
- 7 in. (18 cm) of flat flexible elastic

Other materials:

a 23 ½ x 27 ½ in. (60 x 70 cm) sheet of paper for the child's size and 27 ½ x 35 ½ in. (70 x 90 cm) for the adult size, a pencil, a tape measure, a bowl with an approximate diameter of 6 in. (15 cm) and a glass with an approximate diameter of 2 ¾ in. (7 cm) to draw the circles, scissors for cutting paper, sewing shears, pins, 2 safety pins, a sewing machine, a sewing needle, thread to match the fabrics, scotch tape

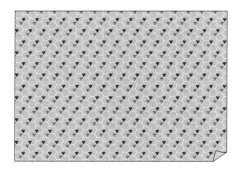

★ **Dimensions without the strings**
Child's apron: 19 ½ x 23 ½ in. (50 x 60 cm)
Adult's apron: 23 ½ x 31 ½ in. (60 x 80 cm)

★ When you buy the coated fabric, do not store it folded. Instead, wind it around itself or around a cardboard tube. This will prevent it from creasing.

SEE THE INTRODUCTION

ENLARGING A PATTERN, PAGE 19 / PINNING, PAGE 36 / SEWING PIPING, PAGE 42 / ZIGZAG STITCH, PAGE 30 / BACKSTITCHING, PAGE 31 / FRONT TO FRONT, PAGE 36

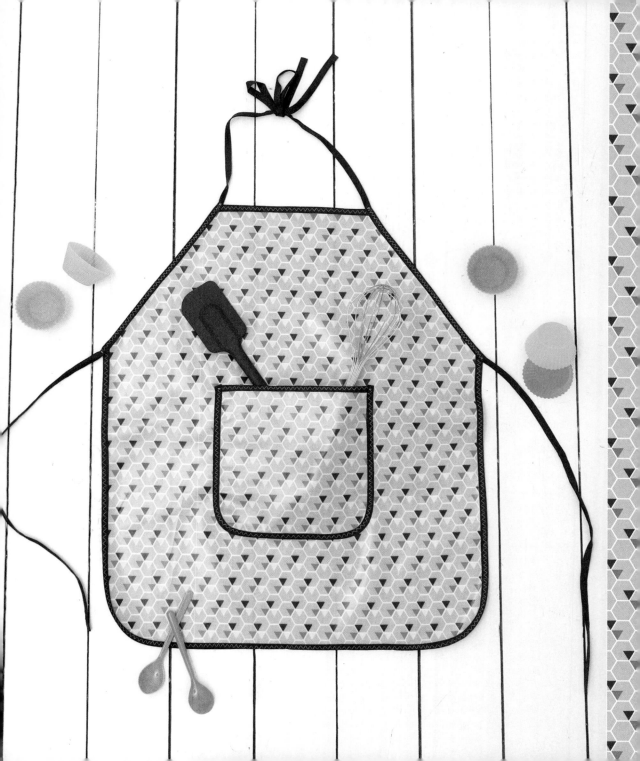

Prepare the pattern

1

Fold the sheet of paper in half lengthwise.

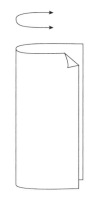

2

See the half-pattern on page 235. On the sheet of paper, draw the grid and, using the reference marks, reproduce the half-pattern.

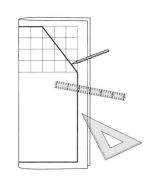

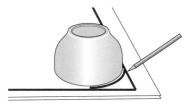

3

Place the bowl on the outer corner and draw the circle.

4

Place pins to keep the pattern closed and cut out the two layers of paper, following the outline. Remove the pins. Unfold the pattern and place it in front of you, like an apron, to check that it suits you. If the pattern is too small, use the adult size. If it is too big, remove ¾ in. (2 cm) all the way around the outline and try it again.

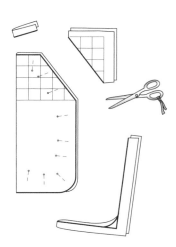

Cut out the apron

5

Follow the cutting guide so that you have enough coated fabric for the pocket, the headband and the scrunchie.

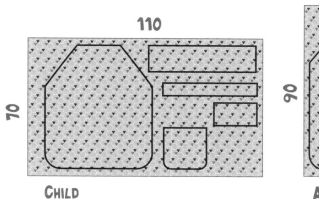

CHILD

ADULT

Place your pattern on the coated fabric, paying attention to the direction of the patterns, and attach it using a few pieces of scotch tape.

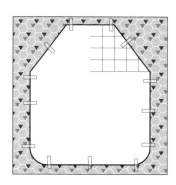

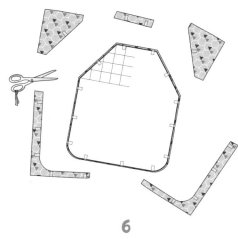

6

Passing over the pieces of scotch tape, cut out the coated fabric, following the outlines carefully to lose as few scraps as possible.

Place the piping

7

Cut a 8 ¾ in. (22 cm) (child size) or 10 ½ in. (27 cm) (adult size) piece of piping and place it front to front on the top of the apron, leaving some extra on each side. Pin it, baste it, and sew it using the machine, ⅛ in. (3 mm) from the edge.

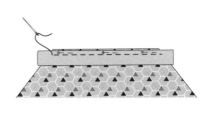
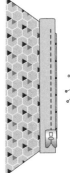

Fold down the piping on the back, pin it and baste it on the middle.

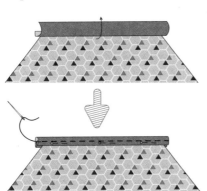

Sew the piping using a zigzag stitch on top of the basting, without backstitching.

8

Cut off the excess piping on each side.

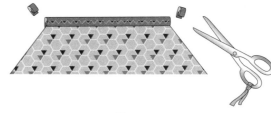

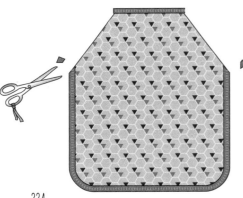

9

Cut a 53 ¼ in. (135 cm) (child size) or 68 ¾ in. (175 cm) (adult size) piece of piping and place it like before on the bottom of the apron.

10

Cut two 51 ¼ in. (130 cm) (child size)
or 55 ¼ in. (140 cm) (adult size) pieces of piping
for the sides. Fold a hem at both ends
of each piece of piping.

11

Place the pipings for the sides of the apron
front to front, leaving about 19 ½ in. (50 cm) of
excess at each end. Pin, baste, then sew.

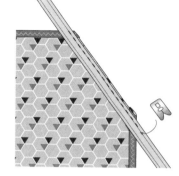

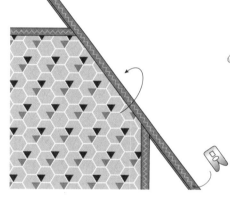

12

Fold the piping, forming the end hems again.
Make the second zigzag hem over the entire
length of the piping, to sew it on itself. Begin
and finish the seams at the hems with
backstitching.

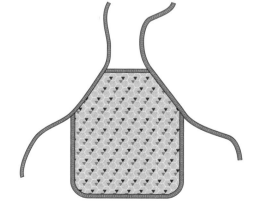

Advice

TO SEW
COATED FABRIC, ALWAYS CHOOSE
THE LONGEST POSSIBLE MACHINE
STITCHES. SEW ON THE FRONT SIDE, SINCE
OTHERWISE THE FABRIC WILL CATCH ON
THE MACHINE STAND.

Make the pocket

13

From the coated fabric, cut a square measuring 8 in. (20 cm) per side. On both of the bottom corners, draw, then cut out rounded edges using a glass with a diameter of about 2 ¾ in. (7 cm).

14

Place a 8 ¾ in. (22 cm) piece of piping on the top edge, as for the apron. Cut off the excess on each side.

15

Cut a 25 in. (64 cm) piece of piping and baste it all the way around the pocket, on the front side, leaving an excess of ⅝ in. (1.5 cm) on each side. Sew it and remove the basting thread.

16

Fold the protruding edges.

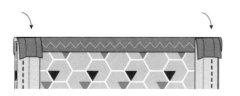

17

Re-fold the piping on the back of the fabric and baste it only.

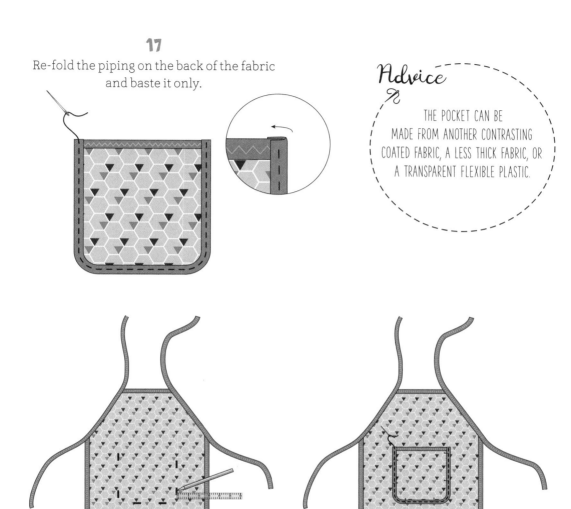

18

To center the pocket, make two pencil marks on each side: at 6 in. (15 cm) from the edges for the child size and 8 in. (20 cm) from the edges for the adult size. Make two marks at 6 in. (15 cm) from the bottom to place the bottom of the pocket. Pin the pocket on the apron (place the pins on the piping to avoid making holes in the fabric), then baste it on the same line as the previous basting.

19

Remove the pins.
Sew all the way around the pocket using a zigzag stitch
on the apron, except on the top edge. Begin and end the
seam with tight backstitching to prevent the pocket from
unstitching when you slip your hands or an object into it.
Remove the basting threads.

Make a matching headband or scrunchie from coated
fabric to hold your hair back while you're cooking...or
when you go to the pool!

Scrunchie

Follow the instructions
on pages 76 through 81.

Headband

1

Cut out a rectangle measuring 17 ¼ x 2 ⅜ in. (44 x 6 cm) and place a piece of piping on each long side, like the apron. With another 8 x 4 ¼ in. (20 x 11 cm) rectangle, make a tube.

Sew a piece of elastic inside measuring 4 x 1 in. (10 x 2.5 cm), following the instructions on pages 107 and 108, steps 5 to 9.

2

Sew the ends of the strip inside after creasing them: sew by hand and reinforce the seam with a few stitches on the machine. First, do a test on a scrap of coated fabric folded in half. If it tends to catch on the machine stand, slip some tissue paper underneath. If the presser foot catches, stick a piece of masking tape under the plate.

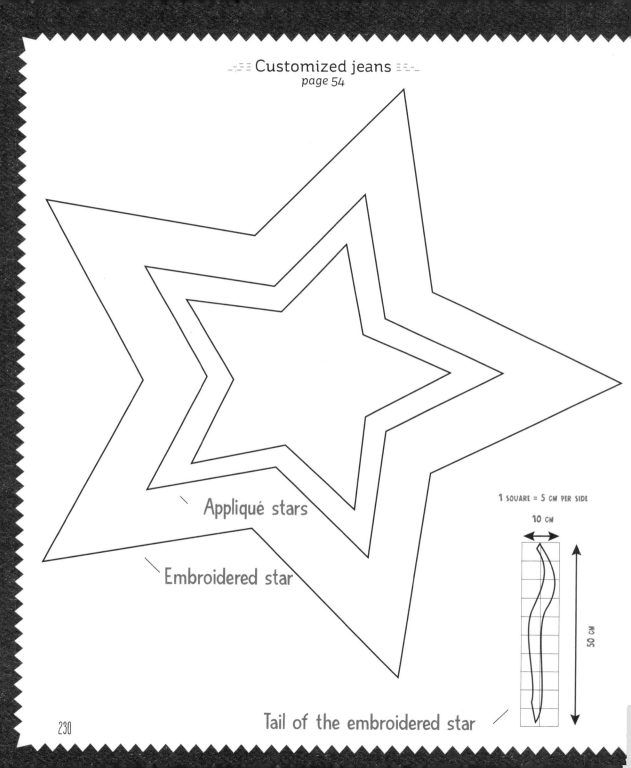

Appliqué stars

Embroidered star

1 SQUARE = 5 CM PER SIDE

10 CM

50 CM

Tail of the embroidered star

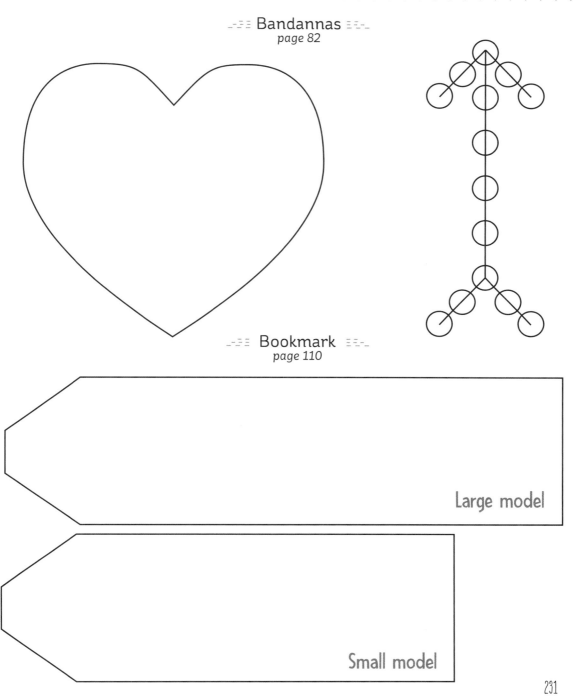

Bandannas
page 82

Bookmark
page 110

Large model

Small model

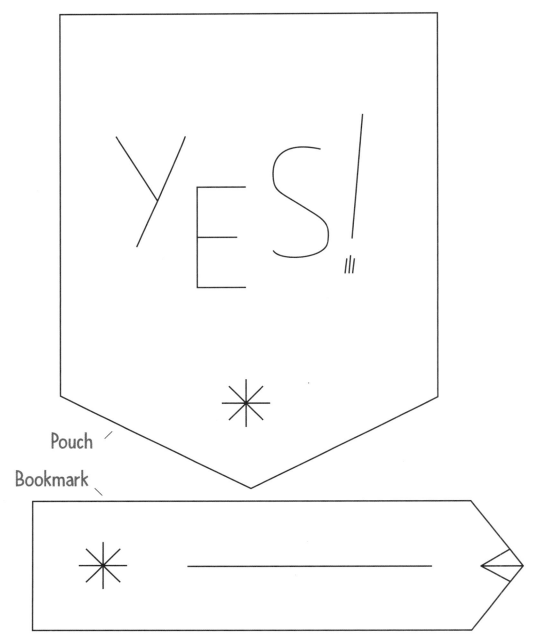

Pouch

Bookmark

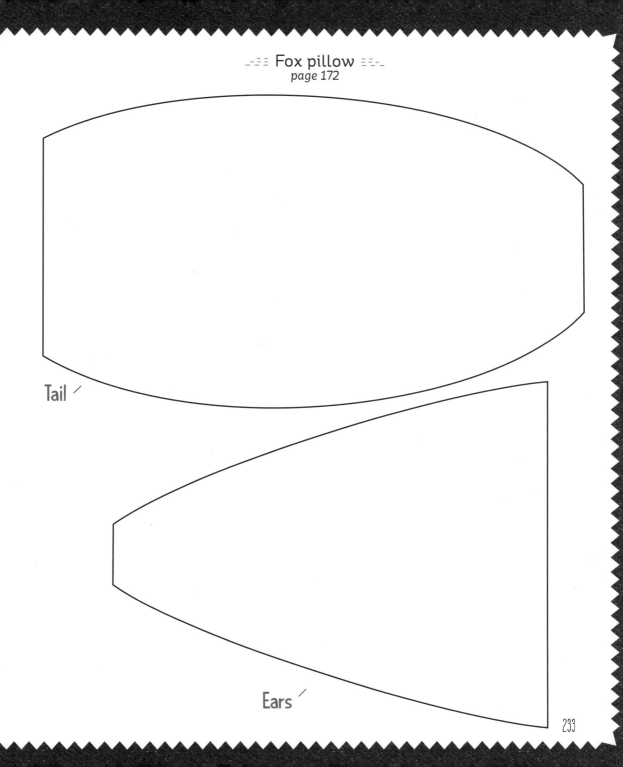

Fox pillow
page 172

Tail

Ears

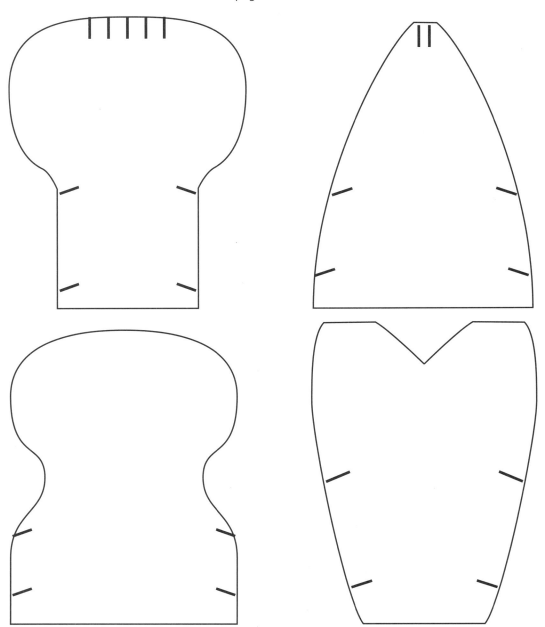

234

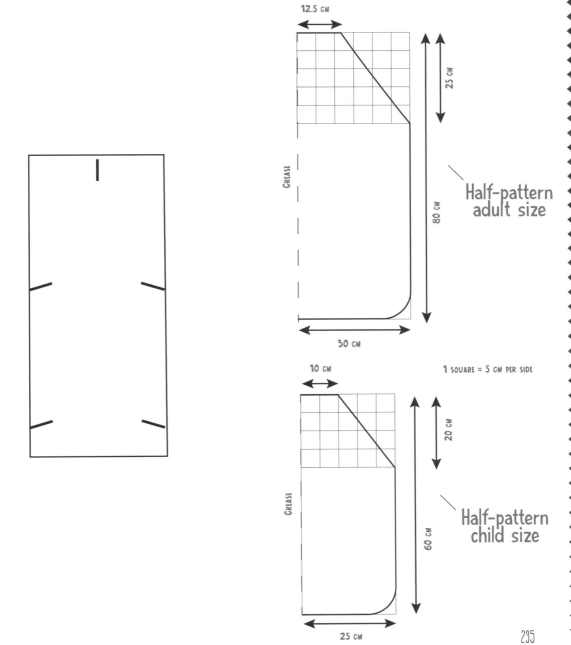

Apron
page 220

12.5 CM

25 CM

CREASE

Half-pattern adult size

80 CM

30 CM

1 SQUARE = 5 CM PER SIDE

10 CM

20 CM

CREASE

Half-pattern child size

60 CM

25 CM

Glossary

Anchor the seam .... Make two or three superimposed stitches to end a seam, by hand or using the machine.

Appliqué .... Small fabric form sewn on top of another fabric.

Basting .... Also called: tacking. Making a temporary seam with large stitches, which can be removed easily.

Bias of the fabric .... On the fabric, line at 45° relative to the selvage. A piece of fabric cut on the bias is very elastic and can deform easily.

Bobbin .... Small flat spool housed below the plate of a sewing machine and on which the lower thread is wound.

Carabiner .... Metal ring with an easy opening system. It is used in particular in mountaineering or climbing activities. Small models are found in fabric stores and hobby stores for attaching charms.

Casing .... Passage in a project, sometimes defined by two parallel stitches, in which elastic or string is inserted.

Charm .... A small ornament attached to a bracelet, a chain, or the pull tab of a zipper.

Coated fabric .... Fabric covered with a varnish that makes it impermeable. (Also called: oilcloth).

Cutting guide .... Diagram showing how to arrange the pieces of a pattern on the fabric so as to use the fabric most efficiently.

Flattening the seams .... Also called: opening (or crushing) the seams. Separating the two margins of a seam one after the other and flattening each side by pressing on them with a fingernail or an iron.

Following the grain .... The grain is the direction of the threads parallel or perpendicular to the selvage. The grain is not very elastic. Pieces of fabric cut in this direction do not deform.

Front to front .... The front of one piece is placed against the front of another piece to make a seam. The back side of the fabric is then visible.

Gathers .... Small folds that make it possible to constrict part of a project, while retaining amplitude elsewhere.

Grain of the thread .... See Following the grain.

Hem .... A fold sewn on the edge of a fabric to prevent it from fraying.

Hem fold .... Part of a hem that is folded on the back of the fabric.

Interfacing .... Piece of heat-activated fabric used to reinforce a piece of fabric.

Notching .... Making small cuts on the edge of the fabric, to give flexibility to a curved or corner seam. This makes it possible to obtain clean finishes when the work is turned right-side out.

Opening the seams — See Flattening the seams.

Overcast — A series of stitches straddling the edge of the fabric to prevent it from fraying. Overcasting can be done by hand, or on the machine using the zigzag stitch.

Pattern — Paper form that is placed on the fabric to cut a model.

Piece of fabric — Bit of fabric cut out using a pattern.

Piping — Strip cut on the bias of the fabric, to be sewn straddling another fabric, to border it. Its elasticity allows it to hug the curves perfectly.

Presser foot — Small piece of the sewing machine that guides the needle and presses down on the fabric to hold it.

Pull tab — Metal or plastic part making it possible to pull the slider of a zipper.

Scraps of fabric — Pieces of fabric remaining after the pieces of a project have been cut.

Seam allowance — See Sewing margin.

Selvage — The two selvages are the edges of the fabric when you buy it. The selvages are often woven more tightly than the rest of the fabric.

Sewing margin — Also called the seam allowance. This is the distance between the seam and the edge of the project. It is generally ⅜ in. (1 cm) or ⅝ in. (1.5 cm).

Slide	Parts of the slide closure with teeth. A zipper.
Slide fastener	Flexible enclosure made up of two ribbons bordered by teeth that are assembled using a slider. (More commonly called a "zipper").
Stitching	Sewing with the machine.
Tacking	See Basting.
Top stitching	Sewing on the front side of a project, close to an edge or another seam.

Conversion Chart

2 mm.	1/16 in.	23 cm.	9 in.
3 mm.	1/8 in.	24 cm.	9 1/2 in.
5 mm.	3/16 in.	25 cm.	9 3/4 in.
6 mm.	1/4 in.	26 cm.	10 1/4 in.
7 mm.	1/4 in.	27 cm.	10 1/2 in.
1 cm.	3/8 in.	28 cm.	11 in.
1.5 cm.	5/8 in.	29 cm.	11 1/2 in.
2 cm.	3/4 in.	30 cm.	12 in.
2.5 cm.	1 in.	31 cm.	12 1/4 in.
3 cm.	1 1/8 in.	32 cm.	12 1/2 in.
4 cm.	1 1/2 in.	33 cm.	13 in.
5 cm.	2 in.	34 cm.	13 1/2 in.
6 cm.	2 3/8 in.	35 cm.	13 3/4 in.
7 cm.	2 3/4 in.	36 cm.	14 in.
8 cm.	3 1/8 in.	37 cm.	14 1/2 in.
9 cm.	3 1/2 in.	38 cm.	15 in.
10 cm.	4 in.	39 cm.	15 1/4 in.
11 cm.	4 1/4 in.	40 cm.	16 in.
12 cm.	4 3/4 in.	45 cm.	17 3/4 in.
13 cm.	5 1/4 in.	50 cm.	19 1/2 in.
14 cm.	5 1/2 in.	55 cm.	21 1/2 in.
15 cm.	6 in.	60 cm.	23 1/2 in.
16 cm.	6 1/4 in.	65 cm.	25 1/2 in.
17 cm.	6 3/4 in.	70 cm.	27 1/2 in.
18 cm.	7 in.	75 cm.	29 1/2 in.
19 cm.	7 1/2 in.	80 cm.	31 1/2 in.
20 cm.	8 in.	85 cm.	33 1/2 in.
21 cm.	8 1/4 in.	90 cm.	35 1/2 in.
21.5 cm.	8 1/2 in.	1 m.	3 ft. 3 1/4 in.
22 cm.	8 3/4 in.		